THIS BOOK
BELONGS TO

♥ Ren ★

♥ Savage ★

GOOD NIGHT STORIES FOR REBEL GIRLS

FOREWORD BY BINDI IRWIN

100 Inspiring Young Changemakers

REBEL GIRLS

Good Night Stories for Rebel Girls and all other Rebel Girls titles are available for bulk purchase for sale promotions, premiums, fundraising, and educational needs. For details, write to sales@rebelgirls.com.

Rebel Girls, Inc.
421 Elm Ave.
Larkspur, CA 94939
www.rebelgirls.com

This is a work of creative nonfiction. It is a collection of heartwarming and thought-provoking bedtime stories inspired by the lives and adventures of more than 100 heroic women. It is not an encyclopedic account of the events and accomplishments of their lives.

Art director: Giulia Flamini
Cover and graphics designer: Kristen Brittain
Editors: Jess Harriton and Maithy Vu
Foreword: Bindi Irwin
Contributors: Ama Kwarteng, Avery Girion, Emily Conner, Frances Thomas, Jess Harriton, Maithy Vu, Sam Guss, Shannon Jade, Shelbi Polk, Sofía Aguilar, Story Hemi-Morehouse, Sydnee Monday, Tatyana White-Jenkins
Special thanks: Grace Srinivasiah, Marina Asenjo, Sarah Parvis

Printed in China
First Edition: September 2022
10 9 8 7 6 5 4 3 2 1

ISBN: 978-1-953424-34-1
LCCN: 2022938063

FSC
www.fsc.org
MIX
Paper from
responsible sources
FSC® C169965

To the Rebel Girls of the world:

Follow what ignites your imagination

and fuels your spirit.

Think big, create fearlessly,

and break down doors.

You are the change.

CONTENTS

FOREWORD

I'm a Wildlife Warrior with a mission to stand up and speak for those who cannot speak for themselves. My life has always been "wild." I live in the middle of an enormous sanctuary called Australia Zoo, and my entire existence revolves around conservation. It's not just what I do, it is who I am. Growing up, my parents filmed hundreds of episodes for a documentary series called *The Crocodile Hunter*. They set out to educate and inspire the world to love and respect all creatures. They involved me in their conservation missions and taught me to treat every living being the way I would wish to be treated. It's essential to remember that a spider deserves just as much appreciation as an elephant.

I joined the family tradition of using our platform to spread the message of conservation by filming many television shows and movies, writing books, giving talks, working with journalists, and utilizing social media. Today, the empathy my parents taught me to have for each species continues on in everything I do. I'm proud to be part of a global initiative to protect our Mother Earth.

Wildlife, wild places, and humans are all connected. When people hear the word *conservation*, they often only think about woodland creatures. However, conservation is ultimately about us, people. The impact we have on our planet will be felt far into the future. That's why it's so important to be thoughtful about how we treat the natural world. Even little things, like turning off the tap while you brush your teeth or planting a tree, make a big difference.

My family and I have created endangered species breeding programs here at Australia Zoo and protected nearly half a million acres of conservation property across Australia. Our charity, Wildlife Warriors, aids in animal crises and human/animal conflicts. We built one of the busiest wildlife hospitals in the world, giving more than 100,000 animals a second chance at life in the wild. I've been on more animal rescues than I can count, and every day I feel a sense of urgency to do all I can for our planet. It's important to me to protect individual animals, while also creating change on a larger scale for our natural environment.

Being a changemaker is about believing in your strength to change the world. I love this book so much because it highlights extraordinary girls and young women who are standing up for what they believe in, to create a brighter future for the generations to come. Entrepreneurs, conservationists, inventors, scientists—there are so many phenomenal life journeys to read about here. Their achievements remind us that it is just as important to persevere with your own actions as it is to encourage others. Helena Gualinga has ignited a movement of activism against all odds because of her strength and determination to make a difference. Esther Okade shows us that you can follow your dreams to undertake and accomplish anything—even advanced mathematics—no matter your age. JoJo Siwa leads by example, by staying true to herself and reminding us all that love is love, always. This book is filled with visionaries who are proof that you can move mountains when you are dedicated and passionate.

As you read about these remarkable trailblazers, remember that you too can be a changemaker with your actions every day. I want you to know that you are exactly what this world needs. The kindness you show to others, the dreams you are passionate about, and the endeavors you undertake on a daily basis are all creating change. Let the stories in this book remind you: the world is yours to inspire.

Bindi

Bindi Irwin

INTRODUCTION

Hi there, Rebels!

This bright and enchanting book is the fifth volume of the Good Night Stories for Rebel Girls series. We are Jess and Maithy, the editors of this special project, and we are so excited to tell you all about it. As you may know, Rebel Girls' books have always featured women from the past and present. But this time, we thought we'd do something new. We've chosen to showcase the changemakers of today—the ones who are building our future right now by innovating, exploring, creating, and leading.

Over the years, readers like you have sent us names of amazing Rebels you hoped to see among the pages of our books. We scoured the hundreds and hundreds of trailblazers suggested to us and were struck by the amount of young women and girls living boldly and courageously. That's when we decided it made sense to tell their stories—and to have them written and illustrated by fellow young people.

First, we picked out an incredible, diverse group of changemakers to share with our readers. We spent months researching dreamers and doers in all different corners of the world, including countries we've never featured in our books before, such as Indonesia, Denmark, Liechtenstein, Bulgaria, Uruguay, and Sri Lanka. Finally, we asked YOU what topics are closest to your heart. You gave us insightful answers and shared your interest in reading about mental health, animal rights, and body positivity. So we made sure to include people like Te Manaia Jennings, a painter who uses her artwork to help normalize mental health discussions; Earyn McGee, a herpetologist who educates people about lizards through social media; and Megan Jayne Crabbe, who inspires others to love their bodies no matter their shape or size.

As you flip through these pages, you'll learn about artists, inventors, athletes, activists, scientists, and more. Some of these Rebels are pushing boundaries in their chosen fields, like Marine Serre, a fashion designer who uses recycled material to make her clothing, or Puisand Lai, who decided that being great at one wheelchair sport just wasn't enough. Then there are those who are carving out completely new paths, like Alina Morse, the teenage CEO of her own healthy candy company, and Shaine Kilyun, whose passion for helping animals led her to create a pet wheelchair business from the ground up. All of these Rebels know that the possibilities are endless for them—and for you!

The subjects of this book are changing the world in real time as they concentrate on unique issues affecting kids and teens today. After seeing a classmate being bullied online, Milena Radoytseva was spurred into action to create an anti-bullying campaign with the hope that, one day, no child will open their phone or computer to find unkind messages. When Rayouf Alhumedhi noticed there wasn't an emoji that looked like her—and the millions of girls out there who wear hijabs— she took matters into her own hands and designed it herself.

We hope each of these stories inspires you to think BIG no matter your age. Cassidy Crowley and Mikaila Ulmer started their own businesses before they hit their teens. DJ Switch Ghana is proof that confidence and dedication (and maybe a funky beat!) are far more important than the age on your birth certificate. And domino artist Lily Hevesh shows us that your unique hobby can turn into something you never thought possible.

Thirteen authors and editors aged 30 and under brought these stories to life on the page in our whimsical fairy tale style. In addition, 82 young artists (as young as 11 years old!) illuminated each subject in vibrant color, using their own distinct tone and medium. This book is proof that when young women and girls come together, magic can happen.

And let's not forget—for the Rebels featured, this is only the beginning of their stories. We're thrilled to capture a small part of their journeys, and we can't wait to watch them grow and learn and DO! Just like you, they have so much more life ahead of them to discover, create, invent, and inspire. And just like them, YOU have the power to make a difference. With your brilliance, bravery, and vision, the future will be brighter than ever. We can't wait to see how you'll shine.

Dream impossible things,

Jess and Maithy

Jess Harriton and Maithy Vu

Download the Rebel Girls app to hear longer stories about some of the inspiring changemakers in this book. You will also unlock creative activities and discover stories of other trailblazing women. Whenever you come across a QR code, scan it, and you'll be whisked away on an audio adventure.

Good Night Stories for Rebel Girls

A'JA WILSON

BASKETBALL PLAYER

Once there was an 11-year-old girl in South Carolina who loved the sound her basketball made when it sailed through the net. *Swish!* It was a familiar sound. A'ja's dad had played professionally overseas for 10 years. So she grew up hearing that *swish* and hearing all about basketball.

A'ja was having a tough time in middle school. Her dyslexia was a struggle, and her confidence was sinking. "I was dealing with self-esteem issues," A'ja said. "I was a tall, lanky, freckle-faced teenager trying to understand where I fit." As she dribbled a basketball up and down the court with ease, A'ja found where she truly belonged.

In high school A'ja earned a spot on the varsity team at 14 years old. Afternoons were filled with sweaty practices, sneakers squeaking on the gym floor, and *swish* after *swish* of the basketball net. College scouts started to take notice of A'ja's speed, skill, and stunning three-pointers.

A'ja decided to go to the University of South Carolina where she helped her team win a national championship. After college, she was drafted to the WNBA's Las Vegas Aces, where she was named an MVP. Basketball took A'ja to places like Russia, China, and Lithuania. She even won an Olympic gold medal in 2021!

A'ja still remembers what it was like to feel out of place in middle school. She founded the A'ja Wilson Foundation to help children struggling with dyslexia and empower them to reach their full potential.

BORN AUGUST 8, 1996
UNITED STATES OF AMERICA

"YOU DON'T HAVE TO KNOCK ANYONE OFF THEIR GAME TO WIN YOURS."
—A'JA WILSON

ILLUSTRATION BY
DANIELLE ELYSSE MANN

AJ CLEMENTINE

LGBTQIA+ ACTIVIST AND MODEL

There once was a girl named AJ who realized that her story had the power to make a difference. But first she would have to find who she truly was.

AJ was assigned male at birth. At home, with her mom and stepdad, AJ was free to play with any kind of toy: water guns, trucks, dolls, and dress-up clothes, or anything she wanted. She could be herself. Out in the world, things weren't so carefree. As she grew up, she discovered why.

I'm a girl, she realized.

AJ was transgender. At first, it was difficult for AJ to talk about her experiences. Some people didn't believe her when she told them. But she didn't let anyone hold her back. She began posting on social media about her journey as she transitioned. *By using my voice, I can help other transgender people feel confident*, she thought.

Slowly, more and more people discovered AJ's videos about what it was like to be transgender. Viewers were attracted to her openness—*and* her colorful makeup and personal style. When AJ partnered with a major LGBTQIA+ festival in Sydney, Australia, things really took off! Suddenly, she was in a studio modeling comfy underwear and socks as the first transgender model to represent a major Australian clothing brand. Then came the book deal. In her memoir, AJ shared her whole story with her fans and encouraged them to share their own journeys. She knows firsthand that one story can uplift countless others.

BORN MARCH 14, 1996

AUSTRALIA

ILLUSTRATION BY
BETSY FALCO

"WE SHOULD BE
CREATING ENVIRONMENTS
WHERE KIDS FEEL THAT
THEY'RE OKAY EXACTLY
AS THEY ARE."
—AJ CLEMENTINE

ALEXANDRA HUYNH

POET

Once upon a time in the busy city of Sacramento, California, a young girl named Alexandra fell in love with words. Growing up, Alexandra spent her free time singing. But she thought the songs in her lessons were a bit boring. *Why can't I just write my own lyrics?* Alexandra asked herself.

She grabbed some paper and a pen, and let the words flow. Writing felt as natural as breathing—it was what she was born to do. Alexandra began to perform her poems on stage. As she prepared for her first citywide slam poetry event, she felt a wave of nervousness wash over her. Could she really share her poems with so many people? She called her twin sister, Brianna, for a pep talk. Brianna knew just what to say. Alexandra stepped out into the spotlight and nailed it!

Soon she was sharing her poems about community, family, and social justice on stages all over the country. In a poem that touches on climate change, she wrote: "The forest is a city with wildfire for veins and a steady churn of smog." Her ability to paint pictures with words and her passion for speaking up earned her an impressive title. In 2021, Alexandra was named the national youth poet laureate of the United States.

As the proud daughter of Vietnamese immigrants, she often thinks about how family and community shape her voice. Excited about her new position, she said, "I'm standing on the shoulders of my ancestors and all the sacrifices and wisdom that they've gained to bring me here." Alexandra hopes all young people share their stories too.

BORN NOVEMBER 11, 2002
UNITED STATES OF AMERICA

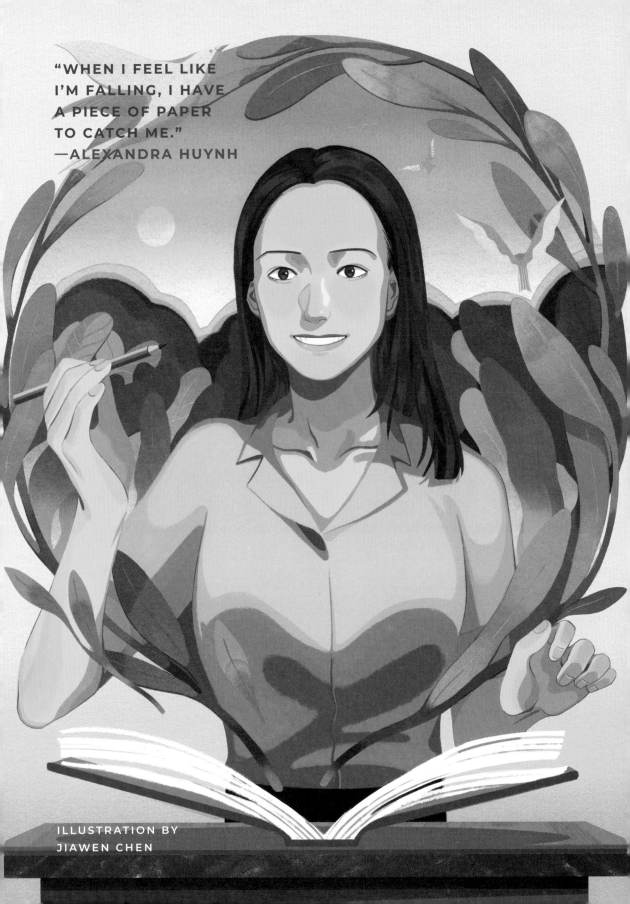

"WHEN I FEEL LIKE I'M FALLING, I HAVE A PIECE OF PAPER TO CATCH ME."
—ALEXANDRA HUYNH

ILLUSTRATION BY JIAWEN CHEN

ALINA MORSE

CANDYMAKER AND ENTREPRENEUR

One day, sitting at the bank with her dad, seven-year-old Alina was offered a lollipop from the teller. She was happy to have the treat, but before she could pop it into her mouth, her dad stopped her. He said that she couldn't have it because sugar is bad for her teeth.

"Well, why can't we make a healthy lollipop that's good for my teeth?" Alina asked. This offhand question would take her down a path she never thought possible.

Alina and her dad began experimenting with ways to make healthy candy. At first, their attempts failed. With sticky taffy on their hands and sugar in their hair, they made crazy messes in their kitchen. Alina asked her friends to try an early batch of lollipops, and they concluded that the suckers were, sadly, sucky.

But Alina refused to let that stop her. She and her dad talked to dentists and tried out a bunch of healthy sweeteners. Finally, when Alina was nine, they found their perfect recipe and created a business. Alina's little sister helped with the name: Zolli Candy.

At 16, Alina was the CEO of one of the fastest-growing companies in the country. Zolli Candy makes lollipops, gumdrops, taffy, caramel, and chocolate that can be bought in stores across the nation. Her adventures in candy-making and business have taken her to many cool places, from the White House to TV talk shows and beyond. It's a pretty sweet gig!

BORN MAY 8, 2005
UNITED STATES OF AMERICA

"I'M JUST A KID FROM MICHIGAN WHO HAD AN IDEA AND DECIDED TO RUN WITH IT."
—ALINA MORSE

ILLUSTRATION BY
EMMA ROSE
ENCOMIENDA ACOSTA

ALMA DEUTSCHER

MUSICIAN AND COMPOSER

Once there was a little girl who heard music everywhere. Melodies played in her head as she lay in bed dreaming or jumped rope in her yard. Alma liked to think the music was coming from imaginary composers in a faraway, magical land. In reality, the songs were coming from her own brilliant mind.

Alma was four years old when she began playing songs for her parents on the piano. They were amazed. Like writing a fairy tale, she was creating something beautiful from nothing at all. They searched to find a special teacher who believed in her gift. Finally, they found a composer in Switzerland. Through their computers, the pair would play together thousands of miles apart. Over time, Alma honed her skills.

She wrote music for the piano and violin and even for full orchestras. Soon people were flocking to concert halls to hear the tiny golden-haired composer play the music that came to her in her dreams.

When Alma wrote her first opera at the age of nine, she decided to adapt her favorite story, *Cinderella*. In her version, though, there was no glass slipper. Alma's Cinderella was a composer, just like her. And her prince traveled all over the kingdom looking for the girl who could finish a melody Cinderella had written.

Critics called Alma the next Mozart. But Alma has no interest in being the next anything. "I think for me it's more interesting to be Alma," she says. After all, she's always been one to write her own story.

BORN FEBRUARY 19, 2005

UNITED KINGDOM

"I'M REALLY HAPPY THAT I WAS BORN NOW, WHEN GIRLS ARE ALLOWED TO DEVELOP THEIR TALENTS."
—ALMA DEUTSCHER

ILLUSTRATION BY CAMELIA PHAM

AMBER YANG

COMPUTER SCIENTIST AND ENTREPRENEUR

While other kids flocked to Disney World, young Amber visited the Kennedy Space Center every weekend. Science enchanted her, especially things that were out of this world—sparkly stars, orbiting planets, and spacecrafts that zoomed into the sky.

One day, in preschool, a group of boys were playing with a toy spaceship. Amber wanted to pretend to be an astronaut, but the boys said that was impossible since she was a girl. It was not the only time Amber was told she couldn't do something. When she joined a robotics team in middle school, a male student said, *Do you even know how to do anything? You can just sit and watch.*

Amber was determined to prove she deserved a place in science. In high school, while watching a film about astronauts, she gasped when space debris destroyed a spacecraft. Space debris or "space junk" is often a piece of a satellite or other object that humans have left up in space. The idea of pollution in space gave Amber nightmares. So she set out to explore solutions for getting rid of space junk.

After months of research, Amber developed a computer program that tracks space debris to warn spacecraft, so they can move out of harm's way. She turned her project into a company called Seer Tracking. No one will ever tell Amber to "just sit and watch" the boys again.

BORN CIRCA 1999
UNITED STATES OF AMERICA

ILLUSTRATION BY
JANICE CHANG

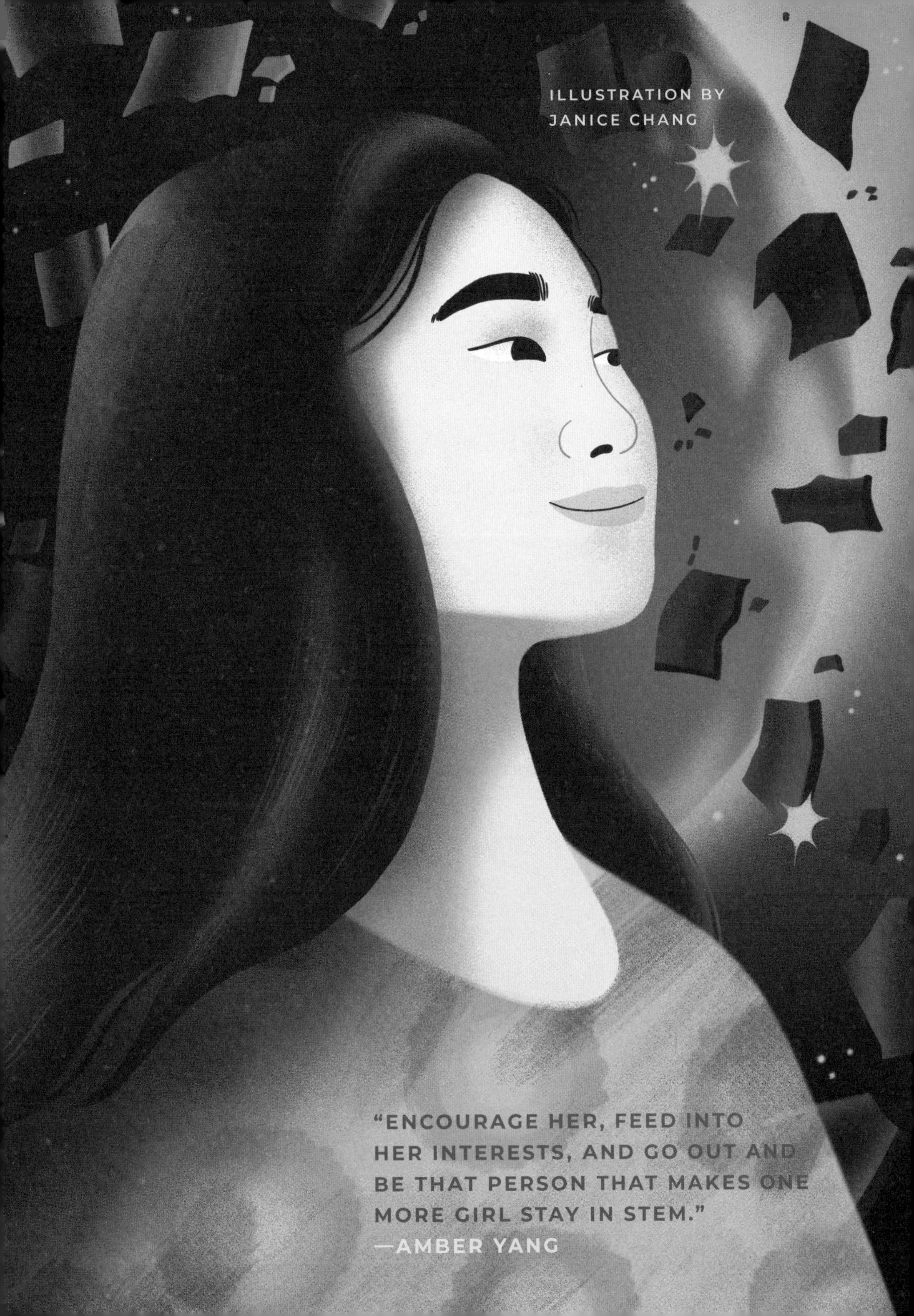

"ENCOURAGE HER, FEED INTO HER INTERESTS, AND GO OUT AND BE THAT PERSON THAT MAKES ONE MORE GIRL STAY IN STEM."
—AMBER YANG

AMELIA TELFORD

ENVIRONMENTAL ACTIVIST

nce upon a time, an **Indigenous** Australian girl named Amelia fought to save the land she loved. Amelia was from a special place located along the northern coast of New South Wales known as Bundjalung country.

Amelia was captivated by all the natural wonders of her home. There were tall mountain ranges and rain forests full of lush trees and hidden waterfalls to explore. Along the coast, there were warm, sunny beaches, perfect places for Amelia to surf and play the days away.

But one day, Amelia learned that the once-pristine beaches were changing. The coastline was eroding and being swept into the sea. And while everyone in the area was sad about the loss of land, not everyone knew how much it meant. Amelia felt that she had to do something. She promised herself that she'd find a way to protect not just the precious land but also the people and traditions that were so deeply tied to it.

Amelia joined an organization called the Australian Youth Climate Coalition, where young activists banded together to search for solutions to the planet crisis. After protesting and volunteering with them for some time, Amelia decided to take on an even greater role.

In 2014, Amelia founded an Indigenous-led organization called Seed. As Seed's national director, Amelia proudly coordinates hundreds of Indigenous activists all around Australia, to protect the land, just as she promised, and to create a brighter future for everyone.

BORN CIRCA 1994
AUSTRALIA

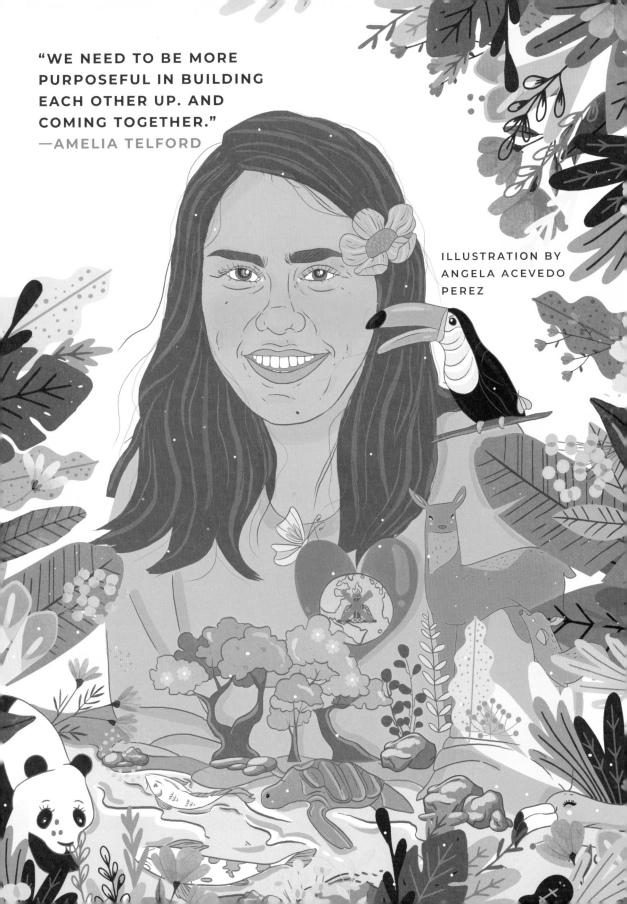

"WE NEED TO BE MORE PURPOSEFUL IN BUILDING EACH OTHER UP. AND COMING TOGETHER."
—AMELIA TELFORD

ILLUSTRATION BY ANGELA ACEVEDO PEREZ

ANGÈLE

SINGER-SONGWRITER

Angèle was born into a family of artists. Her father was a musician, and her mother was an actor. Though her parents were famous stage performers, Angèle never cared for the spotlight. As a child, her favorite thing to do was play piano by herself. She started when she was six and, from then on, her fingers were never far from the piano's glossy wooden keys. There wasn't much to do in Linkebeek, the sleepy Belgian town where Angèle grew up. But that didn't matter. As long as she was playing music, she was happy.

Angèle mastered classical piano and began listening to different kinds of music. She fell in love with the soulful lyrics of Ella Fitzgerald, an American legend known as the Queen of Jazz. Ella's experimental vocals—at times sweet, playful, rough, and romantic—inspired Angèle to sing along. Soon enough, she was writing her own songs.

When Angèle was 15, a friend convinced her to post a video of herself performing. Thousands of people liked it, so Angèle decided to post more. She started joking around in front of the camera: picking her nose, covering her hair in spaghetti, and singing love songs about her favorite foods. Viewers were delighted by her silly, musical comedy.

One of Europe's biggest—and youngest—pop stars, Angèle regularly performs in front of thousands of people. But she still sings for just one person: herself. "I'll always be the girl from Linkebeek who writes simple songs," she has said. "Even if life changes, that will stay with me."

BORN DECEMBER 3, 1995
BELGIUM AND FRANCE

"I WANT TO KEEP IT REAL. NOT TRY TO BE WHAT I'M NOT."
—ANGÈLE

ILLUSTRATION BY OLIVIA WALLER

ANGELIQUE AHLSTRÖM

ENVIRONMENTAL ACTIVIST AND INVENTOR

Once there was a girl who wanted to help nature breathe. And how would she do that? With trees. Lots of them!

In college, Angelique learned that the forests she adored were in danger. She discovered that a major culprit contributing to deforestation is logging. Logging companies chop down lots of trees to use for wood and paper.

Angelique learned that they were using artificial intelligence, powerful vehicles that could operate in rough terrain, and even self-driving trucks so they could reach deeper into forests and cut down even more trees. She wondered why people were using such advanced technology to harm the environment instead of helping it.

She partnered up with a couple of friends from college, and they started a company called Flash Forest. Together they would plant trees . . . with drones!

Once the drones were up and running, Angelique and her cofounders at Flash Forest designed a special nutrient packet full of "secret sauce" to nourish seedlings. They were careful to match the trees they planted to local species, and to plant several species of trees at a time to boost biodiversity. Flash Forest's way of planting trees was 10 times faster than planting them by hand.

Their drones can plant tens of thousands of seedlings a day. But Angelique's goal is bigger than that. She believes they can plant a billion.

BORN AUGUST 14, 1991

CANADA

ILLUSTRATION BY
CATHY HOGAN

"OUR MOTIVATION IS TO
HAVE A TANGIBLE IMPACT
ON CLIMATE CHANGE AND
ALL SPECIES WITHIN OUR
LIFETIME. . ."
—ANGELIQUE AHLSTRÖM

BELLA GANTT

FOOT ARCHER AND CONTORTIONIST

Once there was girl whose toes kissed the sky.

Bella had always dared to be different. She grew up in Pittsburgh, Pennsylvania, where she trained as a contortionist. A contortionist is a performance artist who bends and twists into seemingly impossible positions. Whenever Bella did a handstand or a handspring, her bouncy red curls would do flips with her. People told her that she looked like Princess Merida from the movie *Brave*. So Bella came up with an act inspired by the character. But instead of shooting a bow and arrow with her hands, she did it with her feet!

At nine years old, Bella was invited to perform on a show about young people with extraordinary talents. Wearing a mint-green leotard with sparkly red feathers, she eased into a handstand on stage, wrapped her toes around an arrow's tail, and let it fly. Bull's-eye!

Bella was excited to show off her talent, but while many people praised her abilities, others teased her for her looks. They'd make rude comments about her teeth or her bright hair.

Instead of letting the negative barbs get to her, Bella focused on her future goals. She aimed to one day join a famous circus. Bella developed new tricks—like shooting arrows while doing handstands on a moving skateboard. She also learned how to shoot at a distance of more than 25 feet. With this trick, Bella is on target to beat a world record.

For kids who are being bullied, she has some guidance: keep your head up and focus on what's important to you.

BORN MARCH 6, 2006
UNITED STATES OF AMERICA

ILLUSTRATION BY
MIA JOELY TUÑÓN

"ANYTHING IS POSSIBLE.
DON'T EVER LOSE YOUR
DEDICATION AND
PASSION."
—BELLA GANTT

BENEDETTA PILATO

SWIMMER

Ever since she was little, Benedetta felt at home in the pool. She pushed her body to go faster and faster as she flew from one end to the other. Soon she was competing in major swim competitions around the world. One of the biggest ones was the European World Aquatic Championships.

At the race, Benedetta crouched over her starting block. Her heart was pounding. Hours before, she had broken the world youth record for the 50-meter breaststroke. Everyone at the competition was already talking about the 16-year-old swimmer from Southern Italy. But she knew she could go faster. If she shaved just a tenth of a second off her time, she would break the European record.

When the buzzer went off, Benedetta shot off the starting block and into the pool. Her strokes were so powerful she glided through the water like a dolphin. Right away, the people watching knew something incredible was happening. Benedetta quickly pulled to the front of the group, her candy-colored nails flashing in and out of the water.

Reaching the end of the lane, Benedetta extended her arm out and touched the edge of the pool. The whole arena erupted into applause. Benedetta looked around in awe, raising her hands to her mouth. Then she broke out in laughter. The time on the board said 29.30 seconds. Benedetta hadn't just broken the European record—she had broken the world record!

BORN JANUARY 18, 2005

ITALY

"I STILL HAVE TO REALIZE THAT I BROKE THE WORLD RECORD."
—BENEDETTA PILATO

ILLUSTRATION BY
LUCY NIGHTINGALE

BETELHEM DESSIE

TECH EDUCATION ENTREPRENEUR

Once there was girl who was fueled by curiosity. In her hometown of Harar, Ethiopia, Betelhem's dad sold electronics. Often, Betelhem would look at an object and wonder, *How does this work?* To answer that question, she'd take things apart, then go on the thrilling adventure of figuring out how to put them back together again.

For her ninth birthday, Betelhem asked her dad for money to throw an unforgettable birthday party. When her father said he didn't have any money to give her, Betelhem decided to put her curious mind and interest in problem-solving to use.

She started editing videos, installing software on cell phones, and taking on other small tech jobs after school. Not only did she earn enough money to celebrate her birthday, but she also discovered coding. Coding is a way of communicating with computers, and Betelhem found it magical. She could do all sorts of things like build games and make websites. What she loved most about coding, though, was teaching others how to do it.

As a teenager, Betelhem joined Ethiopia's first artificial intelligence and robotics lab. In after-school programs and summer camps, Betelhem and her team taught young children the basics of coding and robotics. She wants the next generation of Ethiopian students to study tech and learn how their own curiosity can change the world.

BORN APRIL 21, 1999

ETHIOPIA

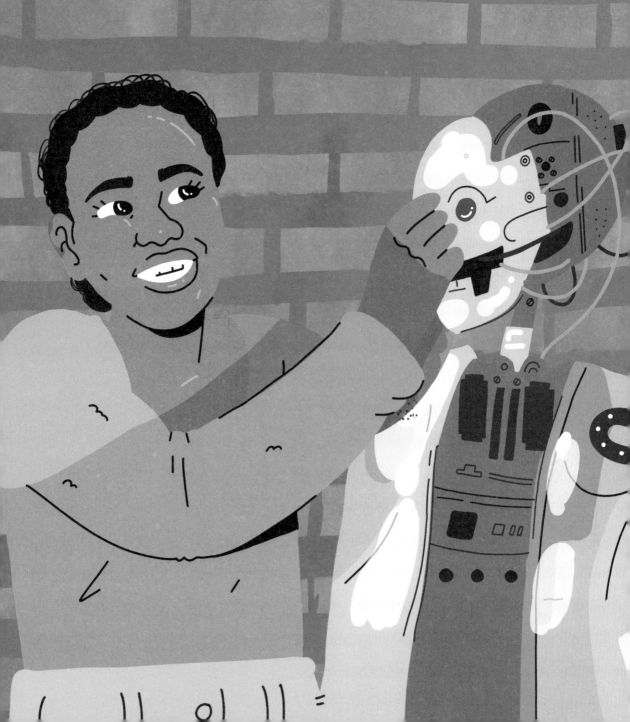

"WHAT DRIVES ME IS WHEN I SEE PEOPLE'S LIVES CHANGE."
—BETELHEM DESSIE

ILLUSTRATION BY
MIA SAINE

BETHANY HAMILTON

SURFER

Bethany Hamilton was born to surf. Growing up in Hawaii, she spent every day chasing turquoise waves under the warm sun. The first time she got on a surfboard, she floated along the waves with amazing speed and grace. It was like she was one with the water.

Bethany won her first surfing contest when she was just eight years old. Soon she was beating surfers much older than her—and it became clear that she was destined for greatness. But first, she had to face an unimaginable challenge.

One clear October day, when Bethany was 13, she went surfing with her friends. The sun was high and bright, and the water was unusually calm. She had no idea disaster was about to strike. Out of nowhere, a 14-foot shark swam up and bit her left arm. It happened too fast for Bethany to feel any pain or fear. Her friends helped her back to shore, and Bethany was rushed to the hospital.

She couldn't stay away from the water for long. After a month of recovery, Bethany was back on her board. Within a year, she was competing again. "Courage doesn't mean you don't get afraid," she has said. "Courage means you don't let fear stop you."

Bethany had to adapt to surfing with one arm, and with a lot of training, she was back at the beach, riding the ocean's crests, curls, and barrels. Her unwavering focus and positivity keep her at the top of her game as a professional surfer. Nothing can keep Bethany from catching her next wave.

BORN FEBRUARY 8, 1990
UNITED STATES OF AMERICA

ILLUSTRATION BY
SARAH MAXWELL

"I DON'T NEED EASY.
I JUST NEED POSSIBLE."
—BETHANY HAMILTON

BILLIE EILISH

SINGER-SONGWRITER

Growing up, there was an unspoken rule in Billie's house: you could stay up as late as you wanted to as long as you were playing music. Billie and her older brother, Finneas, would hang out in Finneas's bedroom and scribble down lyrics, or compose melodies at one of the three pianos in their home. Billie lived and breathed music. She sang in talent shows and idolized pop stars. Still, the whole family was surprised when one of Billie and Finneas's songs, "Ocean Eyes," went viral overnight.

Suddenly, Billie found herself in boardrooms in front of smooth-talking adults who wanted to write and produce music for her. But Billie wanted to create an album on her own terms. "No one listened to me, because I was 14 and a girl," she said. Billie left those meetings and went to work making her debut album the way she wanted to—with her big brother in their home in Los Angeles.

The week Billie's debut album came out, 14 of her songs were in the Top 100—a record for a female artist. She started touring sold-out concert venues and sharing songs about heartbreak and hope with audiences all over the world.

Billie also expressed herself through her personal style. She dyed her hair bright green and wore baggy clothes that she felt comfortable in. Whenever she met young fans backstage, she would tell them to be nice to themselves. Billie knows being a teenage girl is really hard. She wants her fans to know that they're never alone.

BORN DECEMBER 18, 2001
UNITED STATES OF AMERICA

"EVERYBODY ON THE PLANET COULD NOT BELIEVE IN YOU. IF YOU BELIEVE IN YOU, YOU'RE GOOD."
—BILLIE EILISH

ILLUSTRATION BY PAULA ZORITE

BINDI IRWIN

CONSERVATIONIST

Once there was a girl named Bindi who lived at the zoo. She shared her home with cuddly koalas, chirping birds, and slithering snakes. Her dad was a famous conservationist and crocodile expert. She was even named after her dad's favorite crocodile.

Bindi loved caring for animals big and small with her family. One of her favorite parts of the zoo was Roo Heaven, the kangaroo habitat where groups of playful brown kangaroos hopped around in the soft green grass, showing off for visitors.

Bindi's life wasn't always happy, though. When she was eight years old, her dad passed away. She made the brave choice to speak at her dad's memorial. In front of 5,000 fans and 300 million TV viewers, Bindi said, "I want to help endangered wildlife, just like he did."

And she made good on her promise. When she was nine years old, Bindi launched her own TV show, *Bindi, the Jungle Girl*. Through music and dance, she taught viewers about wildlife and what they could do to protect it.

Today, Bindi dedicates her time to the Australia Zoo Wildlife Hospital. She and her team treat all sorts of animals, like Ivy, a bright green baby fruit dove who needed help after she was orphaned. "I'm proud every day to be part of something so much bigger than myself," she says.

Bindi now has a family of her own, and she gets to share the value of conservation with them, as well as her fans. After all this time, the girl who grew up at the zoo is still a Wildlife Warrior!

DISCOVER MORE

BORN JULY 24, 1998
AUSTRALIA

"I'VE CHOSEN TO DEDICATE MY LIFE TO WILDLIFE CONSERVATION SO I CAN MAKE THE WORLD JUST A LITTLE BETTER."
—BINDI IRWIN

ILLUSTRATION BY
ANNALISA VENTURA

BONNIE CHIU

SOCIAL ENTREPRENEUR

Once there was a girl who saw the world through a different lens. Bonnie was raised by her grandmother in Hong Kong while her parents worked. Her grandmother had fled Indonesia as a refugee and never had the chance to learn to read.

Later, Bonnie found out that there were many women like her grandmother—women who grew up without ever going to school. She discovered that two-thirds of the people in the world who cannot read and write are women. Bonnie wondered if she could help make their voices heard in other ways. *Images have no language barriers*, she thought. And she came up with the perfect solution: photography!

A social entrepreneur, Bonnie founded a project called Lensational to empower women and girls by teaching them to tell stories in pictures. Together, Bonnie and her volunteers provide photography training for women in developing countries like Pakistan, Bangladesh, the Philippines, and Indonesia, where her grandmother came from. The women in Bonnie's program capture scenes from their lives, like a canopy of colorful umbrellas at a Hong Kong protest or the silhouette of a pony on a beach in Bangladesh. When the photos are sold, 50 percent of the revenue goes back to the women. Lensational has reached more than 1,000 women in 25 countries.

Bonnie's next mission is to encourage other organizations to focus more on the people they're helping than on profits. It's an ambitious goal, but she's willing to give it her best shot.

DISCOVER MORE

BORN NOVEMBER 3, 1992
HONG KONG AND UNITED KINGDOM

"THE PICTURE THROUGH HER EYES IS THE MISSING LINK."
—BONNIE CHIU

ILLUSTRATION BY JIAQI WANG

CASSIDY CROWLEY

INVENTOR AND ENTREPRENEUR

When Cassidy Crowley was preparing to enter a local science fair, she found inspiration in an unlikely source: her baby sister, Emily. Always observant, Cassidy noticed her mom's brow crinkle with worry when Emily was starting to feed herself. It was important for Emily to learn to use a spoon on her own, but what if she cut her gums on the hard plastic? What if she jabbed her throat? *There must be a better design for a baby spoon,* Cassidy thought. And it was up to her to invent it.

Cassidy got right to work and came up with . . . the Baby Toon! Made from a soft silicone material, this spoon was easy for babies to hold. Even better—it was in the shape of an adorable elephant. The trunk of the elephant could hold only a tiny amount of food, making it impossible for babies to choke. And the square shape prevented babies from poking their throats. When Cassidy presented her Baby Toon at the science fair, everyone agreed that her idea had a future.

After three years perfecting her design, Cassidy took her invention to a TV show for budding entrepreneurs. She and her mom presented the product with big smiles and even a little dance. Cassidy was thrilled when an investor pledged $50,000 in funding to make thousands of spoons! By the time Baby Toon became a real company, Cassidy's little sister was old enough to eat with regular spoons. But that didn't matter. Emily was proud to use the spoon her big sister invented for her.

BORN NOVEMBER 26, 2008
UNITED STATES OF AMERICA

"I LEARNED TO JUST GO FOR IT BECAUSE YOU NEVER KNOW UNLESS YOU TRY."
—CASSIDY CROWLEY

ILLUSTRATION BY IZZY EVANS

CELESTINE WENARDY

SCIENTIST AND INVENTOR

During her sophomore year of high school, Celestine was shadowing doctors in her local hospital in Indonesia when she noticed something interesting and sad. Many of the patients were dealing with issues that were preventable, like complications from diabetes. People with diabetes need to check the amount of the sugar in their blood frequently to make sure the levels are healthy.

Celestine learned that due to religion and other reasons, many Indonesians choose not to have their blood drawn, which is how people monitor diabetes. *Why isn't there a device for diabetic people that doesn't use a needle?* Celestine wondered. She decided to invent one.

She tried out all sorts of methods to monitor blood sugar without a needle. She didn't have a professional lab, so she borrowed what she needed from school. "There were certainly times when I wanted to give up, scrap the idea, and start over," Celestine admitted. But she kept at it. Whenever one idea failed, she learned from it and went back to the drawing board.

After six months, Celestine finally had a working prototype. Instead of drawing blood with a needle, Celestine's device used light and heat to determine someone's blood sugar levels. She presented her device at the Google Science Fair and came away with a prize. Celestine had set out to help her community—the $15,000 scholarship she won was icing on the cake!

BORN APRIL 2003

INDONESIA

ILLUSTRATION BY
KIRAN JOAN

"GROWING UP, THE PEOPLE
AROUND ME, MY COMMUNITY,
HAVE GREATLY SHAPED THE
PERSON I AM TODAY."
—CELESTINE WENARDY

DASIA TAYLOR

SCIENTIST AND INVENTOR

Dasia was in class one day when her chemistry teacher asked if anyone wanted to work on a project for the science fair. Her hand shot straight into the air.

Dasia was inspired by an article she read about "smart stitches" that could tell if a wound was infected after surgery. There was one big problem, though. The stitches required special technology, which made them really expensive. Dasia decided to see if she could create her own affordable version of smart stitches.

She got to work in the science lab at school. The process was not easy. Her beakers broke, she messed up research entries, and she had to spend her lunch periods collecting data. Then she made an incredible discovery! Dasia learned that beets change color when they reach a certain level of acidity. This meant they would change color if they touched an infected wound. After experimenting with different materials, she made a thread that could soak up beet juice. She tested her handmade stitches using acid that mimicked an infected wound. In five minutes, the stitches turned from bright red to dark purple—Dasia had developed inexpensive infection-detecting stitches.

At the science fair, Dasia was the only Black student presenting an invention. She felt a little self-conscious, but she didn't let her nerves get to her—and she won first place!

BORN AUGUST 2, 2003
UNITED STATES OF AMERICA

ILLUSTRATION BY
KELSEE THOMAS

"FIND A MENTOR,
REACH OUT, TAKE
A CHANCE, AND
STAY CURIOUS!"
—DASIA TAYLOR

DEWMINI

GARDENER

Once upon a time, there was a girl who dreamed of growing a magical garden overflowing with mangoes and colorful flowers, and a flowing stream filled with singing fish. Dreaming of this paradise gave her strength to deal with the problems she faced in her everyday life.

Dewmini was born in a poor area of Sri Lanka, where droughts made life very difficult. Some days there was no water to drink, and she had to go to school without breakfast. One day, Dewmini's father decided the only option was to send her to a wealthy house in the city to work as a servant. Dewmini did not want to go. She was determined to stay with her family and help them overcome poverty.

At school, Dewmini learned about agriculture and decided to grow a garden. First, she planted eggplants. Then she added lemons. Then betel nuts. Then okra. Her teachers and parents were astonished—her garden was growing fast!

Dewmini and her father soon began to sell her vegetables to people in the village, and she surprised everyone—including herself—when she won third place in a competition for having the most bountiful garden in the entire district. "It was my happiest day," she said beaming. "I feel quite accomplished to do that at such a young age."

Dewmini has big dreams for the future. After college, she plans to help her town grow even more, so it can have bustling markets, classes for farmers, and plenty of jobs. "There will be plenty of food and drinking water, and lots of trees to give everyone shade."

BORN 2008
SRI LANKA

ILLUSTRATION BY
KATHERINE AHMED

"THERE'S NO GAIN
WITHOUT COURAGE
AND DETERMINATION."
—DEWMINI

DEYNA CASTELLANOS

SOCCER PLAYER

Once upon a time in a small town in Venezuela, there was a girl who was stuck on the sidelines. Her name was Deyna, and she loved soccer. The trouble was, people kept telling her only boys should play soccer.

One day, Deyna went with her brother to his soccer practice. While he scored goals, sprinted through the grass, and played and laughed with his friends, she was stranded on the side of the field. *This is so unfair,* she thought.

When a ball flew out of bounds toward her, Deyna stopped it. Looking at the boys on the soccer field, an idea came to her. She flipped the ball up on her foot and balanced it on her shoe. She kicked it and bounced it off her head. She dribbled it between her feet, loving the strength in her stride. It was as natural as breathing.

Her plan worked. The coach saw her talent and encouraged Deyna's parents to enroll her in soccer. Deyna practiced and practiced. Soon she could run as fast as a jaguar, kick with a hard *thwack*, and score goal after goal. Deyna loved watching the ball arc through the sky like a rainbow and soar into the net with a soft *whoosh*. To her, it was the best feeling in the world!

Deyna took her talents to soccer's biggest stadiums. She played in the Youth Olympics and the World Cup, and she was a finalist for FIFA's Best Women's Player in the World award. And it's all because she had the courage to step off the sidelines and into the spotlight.

BORN APRIL 18, 1999
VENEZUELA

ILLUSTRATION BY
SOL COTTI

"WHAT MOTIVATES ME IS
THE GOAL THAT I HAVE IN MY
HEAD TO BE THE BEST PLAYER
IN THE WORLD."
—DEYNA CASTELLANOS

DJ SWITCH GHANA

DJ

On the west coast of Africa, in the country of Ghana, there lived a girl whose superpower was making people happy. Her name was Erica, but on stage spinning records, dancing, rapping, and singing, she used a special name. "I picked the name DJ Switch because I was switching up the mood of people. When you're sad, I'll make you happy!" she said with a great big grin.

At school, Erica played the drums, laughing and moving to the music in the sun with her friends. Inside, she cooled down and learned with her classmates, raising her hand high in the air when she knew the answers. Erica dreamed of becoming a **gynecologist** one day so she could help women in her area. In the meantime, though, she enjoyed dropping beats as DJ Switch Ghana.

Since embarking on her musical mission, she has performed on some incredible stages. Millions of people have seen her show off her skills online. In 2018, she was the youngest ever disc jockey to win Ghana's biggest DJ competition.

Erica also writes her own songs and releases music videos that get fans on their feet. In "Deceiver," she boogies with her mom. In "Success," she takes the party to the streets and beaches of her hometown. Erica has learned a lot along the way, and she has some tips for channeling your own inner DJ: 1. Practice. 2. Love music. 3. Be excited. 4. Take it seriously. And 5. Have a positive attitude.

With her wise words, anyone can get the party started!

BORN DECEMBER 12, 2007

GHANA

"FORGET ALL YOUR WORRIES
AND LET'S PARTY!"
—DJ SWITCH GHANA

ILLUSTRATION BY
KAMO FRANK

EARYN MCGEE

SCIENCE EDUCATOR

Once there was a warmhearted young woman with a cold-blooded fascination. As a kid, Earyn was interested in animals. She was especially delighted by reptiles. One day, in the rocky Chiricahua Mountains of Arizona, Earyn went on a quest. She had once found a kind of lizard called a Yarrow's spiny lizard, and she wanted to reconnect with her old friend.

When Earyn finally spotted the lizard, it took off like a rocket! Earyn hopped over logs and rocks, trying to catch up. Her little buddy had excellent camouflaging skills, but they weren't enough to fool clever Earyn. She had painted an orange mark on the lizard's back during their first encounter. And there it was! Earyn knew it was her friend as soon as she saw the flash of orange on a tree.

Earyn snapped a picture and posted it online. To her surprise, the lizard's camoflauge stumped folks online—even with the orange mark. Her followers enjoyed searching for the lizard so much that they gave Earyn a brilliant idea: a social media challenge called #FindThatLizard.

Now, every Wednesday evening, Earyn posts a photo to see who can spot the hidden critters. After people find the lizard, Earyn shares fun details about it.

As a successful herpetologist—a person who studies reptiles and amphibians—Earyn hopes to "create pathways for Black, Indigenous, and other people of color to enter into natural resources fields." And she's doing it one hidden lizard at a time.

BORN SEPTEMBER 1994
UNITED STATES OF AMERICA

· 60 ·

"GOOD PEOPLE DOING GOOD THINGS CAN MAKE THE WORLD BETTER FOR ALL."
—EARYN MCGEE

ILLUSTRATION BY SHIANE SALABIE

EILEEN GU

SKIER

Growing up, Eileen loved spending summers in China with her mother's family. But there was one thing that confused her about her trips to Beijing: very few of her friends there played sports.

Eileen was sick of being the only girl on her basketball team. So she invited a couple of friends from math class to try basketball. The next week, she invited a few more. By the end of the summer, she'd successfully gotten all the girls in her math class to join the team.

Of course, basketball wasn't Eileen's only sport. And as time went on, one sport became her focus: slopestyle skiing. In slopestyle, skiers launch into the air and perform spins, twists, and flips. Judges issue scores based on height, difficulty level, and originality.

By the time Eileen was 15, she was competing as a pro. Then she had the opportunity to represent China at her first ever X Games. She was so excited! If she competed and won, thousands of girls in China would see her on TV and discover the wonders of slopestyle.

Eileen crushed it in the competition. She won a gold medal in superpipe and a bronze in the event known as big air. All that was left was slopestyle, her main event. She started gliding down the mountain backward. Then she launched into a series of perfect high-flying tricks. Eileen coasted to a halt, smiling widely. No one could beat her score.

Eileen's life changed in that moment. But she was also certain she'd just changed the lives of little Chinese girls everywhere. She'd given them a skier to look up to.

BORN SEPTEMBER 3, 2003
CHINA

"I WANTED TO INSPIRE MORE PEOPLE TO PICK UP SKIING IN CHINA BECAUSE IT'S BROUGHT ME SO MUCH MORE THAN MEDALS. SKIING BUILDS SO MUCH CONFIDENCE FOR ME—SEEING WHAT MY BODY'S CAPABLE OF."
—EILEEN GU

ILLUSTRATION BY
MARU SALEM-VARGAS

EMMA RADUCANU

TENNIS PLAYER

When Emma set out to play her first match at the 2021 US Open, she had already booked her flight home. She was entering this tennis competition—one of the most prestigious in the world—as a young, unknown athlete. She would have to fight her way through three qualifying rounds just to get to the main competition. Emma was only 18 years old and ranked 150th in the world. She was about to compete against major players she looked up to for years. *Do I even have a chance?* Emma wondered.

It turned out, she did. Emma breezed through nine matches, bursting out of the qualifying rounds and into the finals! There she was in Arthur Ashe Stadium, the biggest tennis stadium in the world. Nearly 24,000 people in the arena and thousands more tuning in at home were about to watch Emma and fellow teenager Leylah Fernandez compete for the championship title.

The match began with a powerful serve from Emma. Sports fans held their breath as the two tennis geniuses duked it out, playing the biggest match of their lives. The ball whizzed across the court at lightning speed from Emma to Leylah and back again. Leylah used her left-handedness and strategic offense to her advantage. Emma was fast, and her strong forehand was deadly accurate. It was a tough match, but Emma pulled through, winning her 10th match in a row—and the title of champion. The crowd erupted, and Emma beamed. She had just made history.

BORN NOVEMBER 13, 2002
CANADA AND UNITED KINGDOM

ILLUSTRATION BY
JOANNE DERTILI

"HAVING TO BE
BOLD ON THE
COURT AND
[BE] FEARLESS
AND FIGHT, IT'S
GIVEN ME INNER
STRENGTH."
—EMMA
RADUCANU

ERÉNDIRA YARETZI MORALES FLORES

HARPIST

When Eréndira was growing up in Mexico, her mom took her to fandangos, where dancers in bright dresses moved to the strums of guitars and the *clap-clap-clap* of castanets. Eréndira knew one day she would play music too, and at six years old, she discovered the instrument she was born to play: the harp. She was drawn to its smooth sound and how it touched people's emotions.

Eréndira began attending a special school for the arts, where she could study harp and dance. Every day she had to travel nearly 20 miles to get to school. Eréndira enjoyed school, but the kids in her class weren't very kind. "I was bullied a lot because *who plays the harp or who listens to Mozart*?" Eréndira says. She ignored them. Every night, she went home and played her beloved instrument.

One day, Eréndira's teacher told her it was time to enter music competitions. Some of these events, like the Golden Classical Music Awards, welcomed performers from more countries than she could count! Eréndira didn't know if she would measure up to all of those talented musicians. She decided she'd be happy just winning third in such a big competition. But Eréndira didn't win third—she won first and was invited to perform at the famous Carnegie Hall in New York City.

Her fingers expertly danced across the strings of her harp, as she played "Au Matin" by Marcel Tournier, a sweet upbeat song. At 13 years old, Eréndira delighted the audience at one of the most iconic stages in the world.

BORN CIRCA 2007

MEXICO

"I PLAY THE HARP BECAUSE I LIKE IT. I DON'T REALLY THINK MUCH ABOUT THE RECOGNITION OF EVERYONE ELSE."
—ERÉNDIRA YARETZI MORALES FLORES

ESTHER OKADE

MATHEMATICIAN

Once upon a time, a bubbly Nigerian British girl named Esther became one of the United Kingdom's youngest college students. On the way, her journey there took a few twists and turns.

Esther started school when she was just three years old, but she did not like her school at all. "They don't even let me talk!" Esther complained. Her mom decided to teach her from home. There, Esther thrived, especially when it came to math. With calculus, algebra, and all sorts of complex equations, she could unravel the secrets of the universe. "All the numbers and the solving, it's like a mystery," she said.

Aside from math, Esther was busy being a kid. She whirled around in a wintery blue dress, pretending to be Princess Elsa. At the park, she swooped through the air on the swings, and on the weekends, she dressed her dolls for brunch dates. But what she wanted most of all was to attend college. At seven years old, she felt like she was ready. Her mom made her wait three years. Esther enrolled when was 10 years old—no big deal for this brilliant girl. "It's easy," she said with a shrug.

Esther created her own series of math workbooks called *Yummy Yummy Algebra* to show other kids how fun math can be. She plans to finish her degree in two years and then get her PhD. Finally, at the age when most people graduate high school, she wants to open a bank. She says it's the perfect combination of her two favorite things: math and helping people. No dream is too big for a girl with a plan—or a pencil and an equation!

BORN CIRCA 2005

UNITED KINGDOM

"I WANT TO SHOW OTHER CHILDREN THEY ARE SPECIAL."
—ESTHER OKADE

$$9x^2 + 15x - 6$$

$$x = \frac{-b \pm \sqrt{b^2 - 4ac}}{2a}$$

$$= \frac{-5 \pm \sqrt{5^2 - 4 \times 3 \times (-}}{2 \times 3}$$

FAREEDAH SHAHEED

ONLINE SECURITY EDUCATOR

Growing up in Saudi Arabia, Fareedah always had her nose in a book. She preferred the company of the characters in her novels over the kids who bullied her on the playground.

When Fareedah was 13 years old, her dad gave her a computer. There was one catch: it wasn't connected to the internet. Fareedah wanted to figure out what made the computer tick . . . and connect it to Wi-Fi. Tinkering with technology lit up Fareedah's imagination in the same way as reading.

Once she was online, Fareedah discovered the world of gaming. It was like being inside a novel as the main character! Fareedah made new friends, but she also realized that there were some unkind people online, just like in real life. She made sure to protect herself by using a screen name in the games she played and never sharing her login information. However, Fareedah noticed that other kids weren't taking the same measures to protect themselves.

Fareedah marveled at how the internet let people travel all around the globe from home, just like books did. She also knew it could be dangerous. So she started her own portal called Sekuva to teach parents how to keep their kids safe online. She filled Sekuva with videos and discussion boards so parents could connect and learn tips about cybersecurity. "We all love human connection," Fareedah explains. "We all love to feel wanted, to belong." With her help, kids' online playgrounds can be full of fun, information, and friends—not bullies.

BORN CIRCA 1998

SAUDI ARABIA AND UNITED STATES OF AMERICA

"YOU HAVE THE ABILITY TO UNDERSTAND AND IMPLEMENT ONLINE SAFETY INTO YOUR LIFE. IT DOESN'T HAVE TO BE SCARY."
—FAREEDAH SHAHEED

ILLUSTRATION BY RAE CRAWFORD

GINEVRA COSTANTINI NEGRI

PIANIST

Once upon a time, there lived a girl who dreamed of having breakfast with Mozart.

It all started when Ginevra was four years old. Her father came home one day and showed her a taped version of the opera *The Marriage of Figaro*. All it took was a single note, and Ginevra was hooked. In no time at all, she knew the whole opera by heart.

Ginevra joined a children's choir so she could be in operas too. She learned how to read music and perform on stage. Soon she was standing on the stage of La Scala in Milan, Italy. The best opera singers on the planet had stood in that very spot, filling the famous opera house with their mesmerizing voices—and filling audiences of thousands with awe. To Ginevra, it was like a dream come true.

When she wasn't singing in the choir, she was experimenting at the piano. She loved the way the smooth white keys felt under her fingers and cherished the many moving sounds she could create—from lively and bright to haunting and soulful. Ginevra began submitting her recordings to competitions. And she started winning.

The world took notice. When she was 10, she got to play for one of her idols, a pianist named Lang Lang. Months later, she wowed audiences at Carnegie Hall in New York City.

Ginevra now records her own classical albums and performs all over the world. She's also hosted a YouTube series interviewing renowned classical musicians—a close second to that breakfast with Mozart!

BORN SEPTEMBER 18, 2000

ITALY

GITANJALI RAO

SCIENTIST AND INVENTOR

Gitanjali was always full of ideas. When she learned that people in Flint, Michigan, didn't have clean drinking water, Gitanjali turned to her parents and said she could help. She was going to develop a special sensor to detect pollution in water and send the results right to people's phones. Her parents raised their eyebrows, not knowing what to say, but they supported their daughter. She entered a competition where young scientists could pitch their clever solutions to real-world problems.

Gitanjali was chosen as one of 10 finalists. She was paired with a mentor to make her vision a reality. She also toured a science lab filled with beakers, chemicals, and busy people in white coats. It was thrilling!

With the help of her mentor, she succeeded in creating her invention: Tethys, a lead detection device name after the Greek goddess of fresh water. It's a fast and accurate way for people to test for lead pollution in their water. Her invention earned Gitanjali the title of America's Top Young Scientist. The girl with the big ideas was just getting started! She quickly went to work on an app that would prevent cyberbullying and a medical tool that would detect whether patients had become addicted to prescription medicine.

In 2020, *TIME* magazine made Gitanjali their first ever TIME Kid of the Year. Not only were her inventions impressive, but they also came from her desire to make the world a better place. As Gitanjali likes to put it, "inventing" is just another word for "using science for kindness."

BORN NOVEMBER 19, 2005
UNITED STATES OF AMERICA

"YOU KNOW THIS WORK IS GOING TO BE IN OUR GENERATION'S HANDS PRETTY SOON. SO IF NO ONE ELSE IS GONNA DO IT, I'M GONNA DO IT."
—GITANJALI RAO

ILLUSTRATION BY AMY PHELPS

GRETA THUNBERG

CLIMATE ACTIVIST

Once there was a girl who made the world listen.

Greta learned about climate change in school and quickly jumped into action. First she focused on things she could do on her own to help the planet: giving up eating meat and dairy, turning off electrical outlets at home, and not riding in planes and cars.

But Greta realized that these things weren't going to prevent the devastating heat waves, storms, and droughts caused by climate change. So she began to think bigger. Greta decided to spend every school day outside the Swedish Parliament House protesting until the government agreed to reduce carbon emissions. For a while, it was just Greta and her big white sign, which read "School Strike for Climate" in bold letters. Slowly, her movement started to catch on.

Thousands of students in other countries organized their own school strikes in the name of climate justice. The world finally noticed the small girl with the big message. Greta was invited to speak around the globe. She even sailed across the Atlantic Ocean, rolling on the waves for 13 days, to attend a climate conference in New York City. There, she asked world leaders to take meaningful action. "The eyes of all future generations are upon you," she warned.

Today, Greta continues to spread her message through speeches, marches, and her Fridays for Future organization, which empowers students around the world to make their voices heard, just like she did.

DISCOVER MORE

BORN JANUARY 3, 2003

SWEDEN

"WE CAN NO LONGER LET THE PEOPLE IN POWER DECIDE WHAT HOPE IS. HOPE IS NOT PASSIVE. HOPE IS NOT BLAH, BLAH, BLAH. HOPE IS TELLING THE TRUTH. HOPE IS TAKING ACTION. AND HOPE ALWAYS COMES FROM THE PEOPLE."
—GRETA THUNBERG

ILLUSTRATION BY PAU ZAMRO

HELENA GUALINGA

ENVIRONMENTAL ACTIVIST

Once upon a time, deep in the Amazon rain forest, there was a girl named Helena. She grew up learning the ways of her proud and strong community, the Kichwa de Sarayaku people. She knew where she lived in the lush green rain forest was special. But in the same year that Helena was born, a powerful force entered her home.

An oil company planned to disturb the rain forest by searching for oil deep, deep beneath ground. Helena and her family were scared. "We value the forest as much as we value people because we believe it has a spirit," she explained. What would it be like to lose the soaring trees that Helena and her cousins climbed? What if the flowing Bobonaza river was polluted by oil? Where would the animals drink? Where would Helena swim?

The oil company and its supporters didn't care about these questions. So it was up to Helena's family and all the Sarayaku people to stop them. Alongside her family, Helena attended protests and marches. She saw her community stand their ground even when the military entered their lands. Their determination led to a huge success in a long legal battle.

By watching strong leaders, like her mother and her aunts, Helena learned just how crucial her voice was. Today, Helena continues to fight to protect the environment and Indigenous people. "I know that this is what I have to do," she says, "give a voice to the people that have been silenced and the people who don't have a voice."

BORN FEBRUARY 27, 2002
ECUADOR

"OUR EXISTENCE IS OUR RESISTANCE."
—HELENA GUALINGA

ILLUSTRATION BY LU ANDRADE

HOLLIE GREENHALGH

CONSERVATIONIST

Twisting webs of silk, eight spindly legs, and blood that runs blue—these are the attributes of a creature everyone knows well: the spider! Some people run away from spiders, but in Cheshire, England, there is one young girl who embraces them and educates others about how amazing they are. Her name is Hollie.

Ever since she was two years old, Hollie treated spiders like friends. She would hold them in her hands and talk to them. On her seventh birthday, Hollie was given her first spider, a Mexican red-knee tarantula. She named her Hairyett—a perfect name for the friendly, fuzzy, reddish-orange spider. On her YouTube channel, Hollie shows off her animals and shares information about them, like how Mexican red-knee tarantulas grow to be about five inches long and live up to 30 years. Along with Hairyett, Hollie now keeps more than 50 tarantulas in her bedroom! She also takes care of snakes, scorpions, millipedes, grasshoppers, cockroaches, and snails.

Hollie believes that if people knew about all the fascinating and adorable things spiders do, they wouldn't be afraid of them. So she shares what she knows, like how spiders clean themselves by licking their legs, just like cats.

When she grows up, Hollie wants to travel around the globe teaching people about animals. The connection Hollie has with animals is her superpower, and she uses it to make the world a better place for all living things.

BORN DECEMBER 20, 2011

UNITED KINGDOM

"I WANT TO SPREAD THE MESSAGE THAT TARANTULAS AND INVERTEBRATES ARE AMAZING."
—HOLLIE GREENHALGH

ILLUSTRATION BY RAE CRAWFORD

ISABELLA MADRIGAL

In the deserts of Southern California, Isabella grew up deeply connected to the stories of her Native American ancestors. Her favorite way of storytelling was performing on stage. But when she was 16, she decided she wanted to write her own story.

Isabella knew that the lives of Native girls were in danger. When terrible things happened, like an Indigenous girl going missing, it seemed like the world didn't care. Isabella was angry and frustrated, but she still had hope in her heart. If the stories of Native women weren't being told by others, then she would step up and tell them. She got to work writing a play about the issues she saw in her community. She called it *Menil and Her Heart*.

Two weeks after she finished her play, she stepped out onto the stage and into the spotlight as Nesune ("heart" in Cahuilla), the sister of a missing girl. She was joined on stage by members of her community and her family. They all hoped Isabella's message would be heard.

Their wish came true. Isabella received two prestigious awards for her play. And, in 2020, she was also invited to speak at the United Nations on International Day of the Girl Child.

In her emotional speech, Isabella named missing Indigenous women, and shared a quote from author Leslie Marmon Silko: "We don't heal by forgetting, we heal by remembering." Isabella reminds people everywhere to not only take notice but also to take action—just as she did.

BORN JUNE 26, 2002
UNITED STATES OF AMERICA

"HEALING DOESN'T COME FROM HATE,
ONLY FROM LOVE AND RESILIENCY."
—ISABELLA MADRIGAL

ILLUSTRATION BY
LYNNE HARDY

ISABELLA SPRINGMÜHL

FASHION DESIGNER

For as long as she could remember, Isabella dreamed of being a fashion designer, just like her grandma. She spent hours flipping through glossy fashion magazines and making dresses for her dolls.

When Isabella grew up, she decided to apply to a fashion school. But there was a problem. Isabella had Down syndrome, which made learning a little more difficult. The fashion university didn't want to teach someone with her condition. Isabella refused to give up. *I know I can be an amazing fashion designer,* she thought. Isabella kept designing and learning. She pinned fabrics, drew sketches, compared colors, and made items like an embroidered royal-blue poncho with tassels and a colorful jacket with flowy sleeves. She used bold colors and patterns that reflected her Guatemalan heritage.

Isabella's efforts paid off. In 2015, she was invited to showcase her work at a costume museum in Guatemala. Her entire collection sold out. Isabella's career had truly begun. The following year, she attended London Fashion Week, where she was the first fashion designer with Down syndrome to show her designs as part of the International Fashion Showcase. With her newfound fame, Isabella created a clothing label specifically designed for other people with Down syndrome.

The university might not have believed in Isabella, but Isabella believed in herself. Her mission to celebrate inclusive fashion was a success, and she can't wait to keep on designing!

DISCOVER
MORE

BORN OCTOBER 23, 1996
GUATEMALA

· 84 ·

"CHANGE A NO FOR A YES!"
—ISABELLA SPRINGMÜHL

ILLUSTRATION BY
ANGELA HIRE

# JALAIAH HARMON

DANCER AND CHOREOGRAPHER

Once there was a girl who got the whole world dancing. Jalaiah could spend hours mixing and matching moves to choreograph lively dance routines. One day after school, she made up a fast new dance where she swung her arms, popped her shoulders, spun her whole body, and bounced to the music. She filmed herself performing it and posted on social media. *Buzz! Ping! Chirp!* Jalaiah's phone blew up as the video was liked and shared. People around the world started attempting Jalaiah's moves. Her dance, known as the Renegade, soon made its way to TikTok.

Suddenly, the Renegade was being performed by professional dancers and celebrities. Every time Jalaiah opened the app, someone new was doing her dance. At 14, she had choreographed one of the most viral dance trends ever. *This is exciting!* she thought. But then she realized she wasn't being credited for inventing the dance.

Jalaiah decided to speak up. Whenever she saw someone doing the Renegade, she posted a comment and asked to be recognized as the original creator. Celebrities and influencers began to notice and support her. Jalaiah became the center of a larger conversation about the importance of giving credit to Black creators.

Jalaiah has since performed her iconic dance on talk shows and at major sporting events. Online creators often reach out to Jalaiah when they haven't been properly credited. She advises them to not let it get to them, but to always "speak up . . . so that people can hear you."

BORN AUGUST 28, 2005
UNITED STATES OF AMERICA

"IT MAKES ME
HAPPY TO DANCE."
—JALAIAH HARMON

ILLUSTRATION BY
TAYLOR MCMANUS

JAZZ JENNINGS

LGBTQIA+ ACTIVIST

One night when Jazz was asleep, a fairy came to visit her in a dream. The fairy was dressed in an elegant blue gown, with delicate wings like a butterfly. She promised Jazz that she would use her magic wand to transform Jazz's body into a girl body. In her dream, Jazz was so happy. Even though she was assigned male at birth, Jazz always knew she was a girl.

As Jazz grew from a toddler to a kid, her parents could tell that she was unhappy. At home, Jazz could be herself. She wore dresses and played with makeup. But outside her home, Jazz felt pressured to act like her classmates thought a boy should act.

After doing a lot of research and meeting with experts, she and her family decided that it would be best for Jazz to transition. Her transition meant that she would be able to live as she truly was on the inside: a girl. Jazz and her family knew her journey might help other transgender kids. So they shared their story on a popular TV show where viewers could see Jazz show off her favorite toys, play with her friends at a pool party, and clown around with her siblings on the beach—just like other kids her age. Almost overnight, she became an icon and an activist for the transgender community.

Since then, Jazz has starred in her own TV series, written books, and given speeches at countless LGBTQIA+ events. "It's about learning to love yourself," she says. She doesn't have wings or a magic wand like the fairy in her dream, but Jazz can get an awful lot done with her voice!

DISCOVER MORE

BORN OCTOBER 6, 2000
UNITED STATES OF AMERICA

ILLUSTRATION BY
AMY PHELPS

"NO MATTER WHAT PATH I CHOOSE, I DO
KNOW ONE THING. I WILL NEVER STOP
FIGHTING FOR TRANSGENDER RIGHTS."
—JAZZ JENNINGS

JOJO SIWA

SINGER AND DANCER

Once there was a girl who lived her life in Technicolor.

From the time she was a toddler, JoJo was bopping to the beat in her mom's dance studio and performing on stage. She developed a style that was all her own, and it was full of glitter, hair bows, and color—*lots* of color.

JoJo's moves landed her a spot on a popular show about talented dancers. Her big laugh and bubbly personality quickly made her a fan favorite. On YouTube, JoJo connected with those fans and attracted new ones. In her videos, she showcased her silly humor by making giant ice-cream sundaes and covering her entire body (head to toe!) in purple glitter. But there was more to JoJo than just sweets and sparkles—she encouraged kids everywhere to be kind to each other.

Soon JoJo turned her love of dance, music, and all things *fun* into a full-time job. She started performing her own catchy pop tunes on tour for thousands of "Siwanatorz" and selling her signature hair bows so fans could rock her look too.

As she grew up, JoJo's inclusive message took on a deeper meaning. In 2020, JoJo shared that she is gay. It was scary to come out, but her confidence prevailed. "I want to be a role model for people who love love," she said. JoJo continues to find ways to make people feel included. On *Dancing with the Stars*, she was the first person to dance with a partner of the same gender. JoJo is proof that with confidence and a little (or a lot!) of sparkle, big dreams can come true.

DISCOVER MORE

BORN MAY 19, 2003
UNITED STATES OF AMERICA

ILLUSTRATION BY JULIETTE TOMA

"I WANT TO LET PEOPLE ALL OVER THE WORLD KNOW THAT YOU CAN BE WHO YOU ARE. YOU CAN LOVE WHO YOU WANT. IT'S OKAY."
—JOJO SIWA

JUDIT GIRÓ BENET

BIOMEDICAL ENGINEER AND INVENTOR

There were two things that made young Judit's brain light up: math and biology. She adored solving equations and learning about how the human body works. She thought she might become a doctor, but the idea of leaving math behind was heartbreaking.

When she was 15, Judit had an aha moment. At a presentation about different career paths, she heard about biomedical engineering. This field combined both of her passions. Sitting in the crowd, Judit felt like two puzzles pieces clicked into place. "Hearing that," Judit said, "was very close to falling in love for me."

While studying biomedical engineering in college, she learned about dogs that can pick up on health issues in humans using their sense of smell. She was intrigued. Her mom had been diagnosed with breast cancer, so Judit knew firsthand the difficult tests women have to go through to catch the disease early. She wanted to come up with an easier way for people to test for breast cancer.

Judit got to work on her invention: the Blue Box, a small plastic box that uses a simple urine sample to detect breast cancer in women. She replicated a dog's sense of smell by creating an "electronic nose" within her invention. The device studies the sample, then sends the results to an app on the user's phone—no poking and prodding necessary.

Judit's invention won the James Dyson Award—a prestigious international award for young engineers. She'll keep improving her design so that one day it can be in the homes of anyone who wants it.

BORN NOVEMBER 5, 1996

SPAIN

"WE WANT TO HAVE A PRODUCT IN THE MARKET, BUT WE ALSO WANT TO HAVE A COMMUNITY OF WOMEN WHO REALLY CARE ABOUT THEIR HEALTH AND THAT REALLY CARE ABOUT EACH OTHER."
—JUDIT GIRÓ BENET

ILLUSTRATION BY JIAWEN CHEN

KAITLIN FRITZ AND OLGA KRAVCHENKO

ENTREPRENEURS

Olga and Kaitlin grew up thousands of miles apart. Olga was brought up in the busy city of Kyiv in Ukraine, while Kaitlin lived with her family in rural Pennsylvania. Though they didn't know it yet, the girls had a few key things in common. They were both fascinated by art and history, they were both described as "bossy" as kids, and they both knew that meant they were born leaders.

The two met in London at a college hackathon. Olga had been working on a prototype for an educational game called Museum 2.0. Neither of them had been planning to start a business, but when Olga showed Kaitlin her designs, the two young women realized that, together, they could transform Museum 2.0 into a product that would help make art and history more accessible for kids who can't just hop in a car or walk to a nearby museum.

Olga and Kaitlin founded a start-up called *Musemio*. Using a smartphone and a simple virtual reality headset made out of cardboard, kids can teleport themselves back in time. Imagine traveling back to ancient Egypt and tiptoeing through a pyramid or blasting back to prehistoric times and feeding a T-rex.

Today *Musemio* is changing the way thousands of kids interact with history and culture, and Olga and Kaitlin are thrilled to be inspiring more young women to pursue careers in tech. Good thing they always knew being "bossy" isn't a bad thing!

KAITLIN FRITZ, BORN OCTOBER 8, 1993
OLGA KRAVCHENKO, BORN OCTOBER 17, 1994
UNITED STATES OF AMERICA AND UKRAINE

ILLUSTRATION BY
ISIP XIN

"I AM PASSIONATE ABOUT
ENCOURAGING MORE
GIRLS AND YOUNG WOMEN
INTO STEAM CAREERS."
—OLGA KRAVCHENKO

KEELY CAT-WELLS

DISABILITY RIGHTS ADVOCATE AND CEO

Keely was always drawn to the spotlight. Growing up, she danced and sang and rode horses in shows. Then, at the age of 17, Keely fell mysteriously ill. Some doctors thought the pain was just in her head, but Keely knew there was something wrong with her body. After a lot of tests, doctors discovered that Keely had a rare condition that affects how she digests food. She had to have surgery, and her doctors attached something called an ileostomy bag to her body to do the work her large intestine used to do. Keely's health improved, but her life changed forever. *The world is not built with me in mind*, she realized.

Keely wasn't ready to let go of her dream of being a performer. During a trip to Los Angeles, she tried her hand at acting. Miraculously, she was cast in a Hollywood film! Before shooting began, she met with the costume designer who gave her a tiny bikini to try on for a scene. Keely felt a pang of dread. The bikini was too small to cover her ileostomy bag. Instead of simply changing the costume, the filmmakers cast someone else in Keely's part.

She was heartbroken. But her disappointment sparked something inside her: a determination to make society more friendly for people like her. Keely founded her own talent agency to represent actors, influencers, and athletes with disabilites. "Hollywood has to reflect the world we live in," she says. She's ready to see more and more people with differing abilities shine on screen.

BORN FEBRUARY 12, 1996
UNITED KINGDOM AND UNITED STATES OF AMERICA

ILLUSTRATION BY OLIVIA WALLER

"AROUND EVERY CORNER
IS AN OPPORTUNITY."
—KEELY CAT-WELLS

KEKE PALMER

ACTOR, SINGER, AND TV HOST

Growing up in Chicago, Keke sang beside her mother in the church choir. She swayed and clapped and harmonized, making music that filled every corner of the church. Soon her mother helped her land a singing role with a local theater.

Acting came naturally to Keke too. By the time she was nine years old, she'd scored her first film role and moved to Hollywood. Her big break came when she was 12. She starred in a major film as an uncommonly clever teen competing in the National Spelling Bee.

But Keke didn't want to leave singing behind, so she recorded her debut album, *So Uncool*. It was a celebration of standing out from the crowd. Her lyrics encouraged people to be themselves.

By the time she was 20, Keke was the youngest talk show host in history! Her show, *Just Keke,* was filled with interviews, pranks, and real talk about everything from dance moves to cyberbullying.

On social media, she raised her glorious voice to speak out about racism, sexism, colorism, mental health, and more. She spoke from the heart about the depression and anxiety these challenges can cause. Sharing her own experiences helped her feel more empowered too.

Keke also launched her own music label, starred in films and TV shows, hosted several talk shows, and even made history as Broadway's first Black Cinderella. But she's not ready to live happily ever after. There are many more feats and adventures to come for Keke!

BORN AUGUST 26, 1993
UNITED STATES OF AMERICA

"OUR GENERATION INSPIRES ME SO MUCH."
—KEKE PALMER

ILLUSTRATION BY
NOA DENMON

KIARA NIRGHIN

SCIENTIST AND INVENTOR

When Kiara was 13 years old, she got very sick. In her hospital bed, dealing with intense pain, she discovered strength she didn't know she had. *If I can endure something like this, then I can do so much more than I thought I could*, she told herself.

Kiara spent her time in the hospital reading tons of science journals. She was learning all the time. And all that studying would pay off. Months after her hospitalization, Kiara was on a road trip with her family in her home country of South Africa. She knew there was a water shortage in South Africa, but she soon learned the problem was even more widespread than that. Driving around, she saw two reservoirs that were almost empty. Without water, their crops couldn't survive and people would go hungry. *How can I help these farmers?* Kiara wondered.

Her brain was whirring. She designed experiments to test out some of her ideas. After a lot of trial and error, Kiara invented something remarkable. Using the peels of oranges and avocados, she created a special polymer, or material, that was highly absorbent. When planted in the ground, her invention could soak up tons of water and keep crops hydrated—even during droughts.

Kiara named her idea No More Thirsty Crops and entered it in the 2016 Google Science Fair. To her surprise, she won! She began developing her technology with a major agriculture company. Kiara's thirst for knowledge not only helped her own health crisis but the world's too.

BORN FEBRUARY 25, 2000
SOUTH AFRICA

"IT'S IMPORTANT TO NOT JUST CORRECT THE ISSUES, BUT SPEAK UP ABOUT STOPPING THEM TOO."
—KIARA NIRGHIN

ILLUSTRATION BY JUNETIEN

KOFFEE

REGGAE SINGER AND RAPPER

Growing up in Spanish Town, Jamaica, Koffee went to church with her mother every week. There, she learned to sing. In an instant, she knew music was her future.

Koffee spent all her free time singing, rapping, DJing, playing guitar, and writing her own songs. Her first big break came when she wrote a reggae song celebrating the runner Usain Bolt and posted a video online. "The sky is no limit, go beyond," the 17-year-old sang. "You're a legend." Usain reposted the video, and it blew up.

Overnight, she became an internet sensation.

Koffee was much too ambitious to be a one-hit wonder, though. She got right to work making more music. She wrote the song "Burning" to remind herself of the fire within her and to inspire others to keep their heads up during tough times. And in 2019, she released her first album, *Rapture*. Full of Koffee's smooth voice and inspiring lyrics, it was nominated for a Grammy award. Koffee was thrilled.

She walked the red carpet in a tailored black suit with her signature locs piled in a bun on top of her head. "I'm excited and nervous!" Koffee said in an interview on her way into the theater. She waited in anticipation as the nominees were called. And the Grammy for Best Reggae Album went to . . . Koffee! She smiled wide, and her braces glittered as cameras flashed. She had made history as the first woman and the youngest person to ever win in the reggae category. Now, Usain Bolt isn't the only legend Koffee sings about.

DISCOVER MORE

BORN FEBRUARY 16, 2000
JAMAICA

"IF YOU HAVE TALENT, THAT'S A START. BUT YOU NEED THE COURAGE."
—KOFFEE

ILLUSTRATION BY
MONET ALYSSA

LAURA DEKKER

SAILOR

Once there was a girl who had a big dream: she wanted to sail around the world—by herself. And she didn't want to wait. She wanted to go *now*.

Laura's unusual childhood began on the water. She was born on a boat, and she built her first raft when she was six years old. At the age of 14, Laura got the greenlight to head out on her adventure. She hopped in *Guppy*, her candy-apple-red sailboat, and set sail.

For most of the 518 days of her trip, Laura was alone. It was up to her to handle the challenges that came her way. Once, when she was sailing through the Torres Strait, a storm rolled in at night. *Whooosh!* The wind was so strong it ripped one of Laura's sails. On top of the gusts and rain, the strait was tricky to navigate because it was surrounded by reefs that could scrape the bottom of *Guppy*. Laura was up all night. Luckily, by the time the sun came up, the storm had died down. Laura was able to replace the sail and continue on her journey.

Even when things were difficult, Laura knew she had made the right decision. She got to explore the volcanic island of Bora Bora, with its white sand beaches and turquoise waters. She marveled at giant sea turtles in the Galápagos and gazed up at rushing waterfalls in Tahiti.

When Laura anchored in the Caribbean at the end of her trip, newscasters from all over were gathered to see her. After nearly a year and a half at sea, Laura had proved to the world what she had known all along—she alone could make her wildest dreams come true.

DISCOVER MORE

BORN SEPTEMBER 20, 1995
NEW ZEALAND AND THE NETHERLANDS

"LIFE ISN'T ALWAYS FAIR, AND NEITHER
ARE THE WAVES AND THE WIND . . .
I LEARNED TO MAKE THE
BEST OF IT."
—LAURA DEKKER

ILLUSTRATION BY
MAJU BENGEL

LEILA HADDAD

BLADESMITH

O nce upon a time in her father's workshop, a girl named Leila discovered the magic of making knives. She would sit on the workbench, watching her dad work with angle grinders, files, and hacksaws. Orange flames darted and glowed as he hammered and pressed the glowing, hot metals. Leila was mesmerized. When she was six years old, she joined her father at the forge and began making knives. She's been enchanted by knife making ever since.

Like the blacksmiths and weapon makers from fantasy novels, Leila uses her magic to make amazing tools for her customers. However, unlike swords that slay dragons and protect kings and queens, Leila's knives are made for chefs, who need sharp reliable blades to chop, dice, and mince.

Leila turns her work into art by balancing beauty and purpose. Her speciality is adding a marble swirl design to her knives. She creates curves and whorls through a process called forge welding, a technique that has been used for centuries.

Traveling around the world giving presentations, she speaks about how good it feels to create something that lasts. "Think of how many hands have touched a knife, young and old," Leila says. "Think of how many Sunday roasts it's carved up."

Much like the blades in any good fantasy tale, Leila's sturdy and beautiful knives will be passed down for generations.

BORN NOVEMBER 15, 2002
AUSTRALIA

"THE END RESULT IS AMAZING—TO GO 'WOW, I'VE DONE THIS.'"
—LEILA HADDAD

ILLUSTRATION BY RACHEL ELEANOR

LIINA HEIKKINEN

WILDLIFE PHOTOGRAPHER

Liina and her father were spending the day with their favorite family of foxes on the island of Lehtisaari in Finland. The baby foxes were growing up so fast! After just a few months, the six cubs were already nearly as large as their mama and papa. They were still too young to venture far outside of the nest to hunt for voles and mice. Mostly, they ate insects and earthworms.

Around 7 pm, the quiet little fox den came to life. The mama fox brought home a barnacle goose for dinner. Feathers flew as the cubs pounced and began to feast. But one little fox decided he wasn't getting his fair share. He snatched the goose away and pulled it into a corner of the den between two moss-covered rocks. Liina's heart leapt. She knew this was a special moment to capture. Carefully, she lifted her camera and *click!* She pressed down on the shutter-release button.

When she developed the photo, Liina was delighted. The shot was incredible. It showed the triumphant cub with his goose prize, his snout crinkled and his eyes gleaming. Liina had been photographing nature since she was eight. And she knew that "The Fox That Got the Goose" was a great shot. She submitted it for the Young Wildlife Photographer of the Year Award and won.

Liina's advice for aspiring photographers is simple: if you are willing to put in the time, you can catch something amazing in action. "You have to work for it, and try again if you don't succeed," she says. Whether you're on a Finnish island or in your local park, there's always something to see.

BORN 2007

FINLAND

"DON'T GIVE UP. KEEP YOUR HEAD HIGH!"
—LIINA HEIKKINEN

ILLUSTRATION BY
JAMIE GREEN

LILY HEVESH

DOMINO ARTIST

When Lily was nine years old, she found a box of 28 dominoes in her grandparents' house and began to play. She loved the *clack-clack-clack* sound they made as they fell, one after another in rows on the floor. Dominoes became Lily's favorite hobby. She never imagined it would be anything more.

But then Lily discovered that some people made online videos of their dominoes toppling and that dominoes could be used to build structures, draw portraits, and even spell out words.

Lily started her own YouTube channel, "Hevesh5," where she uploaded videos of her projects. She learned the tricks she saw other builders do online. It wasn't long before she was creating spellbinding spirals and intricate designs of animals and people. She happily spent hours—even days—placing thousands of dominoes in lines and patterns, tiptoeing around her bedroom in her socks, hoping not to knock anything over. Lily became *very* good at setting up dominoes. Her hobby also taught her a lot about geometry, physics, and design.

Other domino artists began to comment on her videos. And she responded. As her follower count grew and grew, Lily realized this wasn't just a side project anymore. For the first time, Lily appeared on camera, becoming the face of the community she built.

Today, Lily creates domino art for all sorts of companies and brands. What started with a few falling dominoes has turned into a dream job. "Following your passion," Lily says, "is really the best thing you can do."

BORN OCTOBER 2, 1998
UNITED STATES OF AMERICA

"FAILURE IS PART OF THE PROCESS ITSELF."
—LILY HEVESH

ILLUSTRATION BY
EVELYN KANDIN GELER

THE LINDA LINDAS

PUNK ROCK BAND

When a boy at school told 10-year-old Mila that his dad said to stay away from Chinese people, she was confused and hurt. She hadn't realized that some people in the United States were blaming China for the global COVID-19 pandemic. She didn't know how to respond to something so racist and ridiculous. Well, actually she did. One five-hour video call later, she and her cousin Eloise had finished writing the lyrics to what would become the song "Racist, Sexist Boy." Thirteen-year-old Eloise shouted "Racist, sexist boy!" in the song's refrain. "We rebuild what you destroy!"

Their punk band, the Linda Lindas, included Mila on drums; Mila's 14-year-old sister, Lucia, on guitar; Eloise on bass; and their 16-year-old friend Bela on guitar. Because everyone in the band was Asian, Latinx, or both, the girls all had a lot to say about racist, sexist boys like the one at Mila's school. The song was their anthem against ignorance and unkindness. They began rehearsing to perform it at their local library.

A few weeks later, Mila and Lucia's dad barged into their room, interrupting their online class. *Had they heard the news?* The Linda Lindas were going viral on the internet! The Los Angeles Public Library had posted a clip of their song online, and people were sharing it far and wide. The girls were amazed.

They didn't know if the boy in Mila's class had seen the video or not, and it didn't matter. They had something to say, they'd shouted it out loud, and millions of people had heard.

LUCIA, JANUARY 13, 2007 • BELA, SEPTEMBER 16, 2004
MILA, AUGUST 15, 2010 • ELOISE, FEBRUARY 10, 2008
UNITED STATES OF AMERICA

"ALL THESE EMOTIONS
KIND OF BOTTLE UP . . . IT
FEELS GOOD TO YELL
IT OUT."
—ELOISE WONG

ILLUSTRATION BY
JANICE CHANG

LUCÍA MONTENEGRO

WHEELCHAIR RACER

Lucía always knew she'd achieve something amazing. She dreamed of an **inclusive** world where she could shine.

Lucía was born with partial paralysis in her legs, and one summer, while at a summer camp for kids with disabilities, she tried something new: wheelchair racing. She loved the feeling of the wind through her hair as she sped down the track. She loved how strong her arms became from pushing herself harder and harder. Lucía was an athlete in the making.

She focused, trained, and began competing. In 2017, Lucía was ready to attend her first major tournament, the World Para Junior World Championships in Switzerland. She was even invited to carry the flag for Argentina.

The day of Lucía's race arrived. *Bang!* The starting gun went off, and Lucía raced down the track as fast as she could. *I'm going to place last*, she thought.

But she kept pace with the fastest racers. *What's going on?* she wondered. *Why are the others not passing me?* Lucía was too fast! She sped all the way to the finish line, where she received her first silver medal. She won two more in different events during the tournament.

Before her first race, Lucía had never even heard of the Paralympic Games. A few years later, she was one of the fastest junior wheelchair racers on Earth. One day, she hopes to be a Paralympic medalist.

BORN AUGUST 11, 2000
ARGENTINA

"MY DISABILITY AND SPORT LED ME TO DISCOVER A NEW WORLD."
—LUCÍA MONTENEGRO

ILLUSTRATION BY
SELAH POTMA

MAARTJE MURPHY

GELATO MAKER AND ENTREPRENEUR

Maartje spent her early years in the Netherlands on her family's dairy farm. The Netherlands is known for its tall windmills and fields of colorful tulips, but dairy is one of its biggest businesses. Farmers across the country raise cows and use their milk to make cheese, yogurt, and, perhaps most deliciously, gelato.

When she was 14 years old, Maartje moved to North Dakota, but she never forgot the heavenly taste of her favorite dessert. Lucky for her, she would return to the Netherlands to visit her grandparents every year. "We'd visit a gelato shop once, sometimes twice a day," Maartje said. The sweet, cold, creamy dessert was perfect for her summer visits and always made her feel connected to her home country. *Why leave it behind?* she thought.

Back in North Dakota, Maartje told her parents that she wanted to open a gelato shop. At first, the idea seemed outlandish, but when Maartje's mother found a gelato-making class nearby, the vision began to bloom. Dairy farming was a family tradition, after all. So, with her parents' help, Maartje started producing cheese, gelato, and ice cream.

Now Maartje has her own business, Duchessa Gelato, a welcome addition to her rural community. She's made more than 100 flavors, from classics like chocolate and vanilla to out-of-the-box flavors like carrot cake and rhubarb. Maartje travels across the Midwest sharing her gelato from her polka-dot cart at weddings, graduations, and farmer's markets. She's thrilled to bring a sweet taste of home wherever she goes.

BORN JANUARY 1995

THE NETHERLANDS AND UNITED STATES OF AMERICA

ILLUSTRATION BY
ROCÍO CAPUTO

"CHANGE YOUR MIND-SET FROM 'IT'S NOT POSSIBLE,' TO 'HOW CAN WE MAKE THIS POSSIBLE?'"
—MAARTJE MURPHY

MAAYAN SEGAL

PLAYING CARD DESIGNER AND ENTREPRENEUR

Once upon a time, while on vacation with her family, a young girl named Maayan noticed something upsetting about playing cards. She was relaxing and playing a game of gin rummy with her dad, when she turned to him and asked: "Why is the queen card worth less than the king?"

Her dad was stumped. A queen is just as important as a king, so why should their points in the game be different? This was the inspiration for Maayan's creation: a deck of cards that was fun, diverse, and showed a more accurate image of the world.

Maayan was 13 years old when she began designing her new cards. In her deck, kings and queens are equal, dukes and duchesses are equal, and princes and princesses have replaced the jacks. The joker is a woman. She called her card company Queeng and put her decks up for sale.

After releasing the first set of cards, she got some feedback from customers that made her realize she had more work to do. Maayan started sketching again. And soon, she'd created even more diverse cards by including characters of different ethnicities and cultures.

Maayan believes that when kids hold a deck of cards in their hands, they should be able to see themselves. "Games can unite us," she says. "Games have the power to bring us together."

BORN NOVEMBER 26, 2003

ISRAEL

"GOOD IDEAS CAN COME FROM ANYONE. IF YOU BELIEVE IN YOUR IDEA, GET SUPPORT FROM YOUR LOVED ONES AND JUST GET STARTED!"
—MAAYAN SEGAL

ILLUSTRATION BY YEGANEH YAGHOOBNEZHAD

MAJA KUCZYŃSKA

INDOOR SKYDIVER

Maja was 10 years old the first time she jumped out of a plane. Her father, an experienced skydiver, took Maja to try the hobby he enjoyed so much. Strapped to an instructor, Maja stepped out into the sky. She screamed her head off! She'd never experienced anything like that before.

Later that day, Maja discovered the sport that would change her life. After the jump with her father, she went to an indoor wind tunnel. From the outside, the tunnel just looked like an empty glass column. But for Maja, it was so much more. She suited up and stepped inside. Suddenly, a gust of wind shot her into the air high above the ground. Maja felt weightless and free. She wasn't *falling* like she had when she jumped out of a plane. Now she was *flying*!

From then on, Maja trained as an indoor skydiver. She discovered that she was able to use the moves and techniques she'd learned in gymnastics to control her body in the air. Her new sport also let Maja use her brain. Indoor skydivers use physics to pull off the daring spins and flips they perform.

Inspired by ballet, breakdancing, and skateboarding, Maja gets creative as she choreographs her moves. "While in the tunnel," she says, "I can go in and play and create something nobody has ever seen before."

Maja's creativity has certainly paid off. At 15, she won the first-ever Junior Freestyle World Championship. Maja was born to fly!

BORN JANUARY 25, 2000

POLAND

ILLUSTRATION BY
ANNA DIXON

"I ALWAYS WANTED TO FLY."
—MAJA KUCZYŃSKA

MARGARET ZHANG

FASHION STYLIST AND EDITOR

Once upon a time in Sydney, Australia, there was a girl whose curiosity knew no bounds. Margaret loved ballet, but as she leaped and pirouetted, she fell in love with the music of the piano—so she learned to play. The world of dance introduced her to the joy of costumes, and soon she was crafting her own clothing. Even as a child, Margaret knew she didn't want to do or be just one thing.

Growing up, Margaret was influenced by both her Chinese and Australian cultures. She learned to translate between different languages, traditions, and values, and she built an identity all her own. When she was 16, Margaret created a personal style blog. She also began shooting films and experimenting with photography.

While in college, Margaret traveled across the ocean to take photos at New York Fashion Week. She made sure to catch the runway show of Diane von Fürstenberg, a Belgian designer famous for inventing the wrap dress. Inching as close as she could to the models, Margaret snapped her camera furiously to capture their glam-rock looks—the hot-pink satin pantsuits and metallic leather pants. *On the runway, anything is possible*, Margaret thought. *Why should real life be any different?*

At 27, Margaret became editor in chief of *Vogue China*—the youngest person ever to run the magazine. With electric-blue hair and a flair for boundary-pushing fashion statements, Margaret is bringing *Vogue* into a new era.

BORN MAY 27, 1993
AUSTRALIA AND CHINA

"THERE ARE HUNDREDS OF CAREER PATHS THAT ARE YET TO BE REALIZED."
—MARGARET ZHANG

ILLUSTRATION BY CAMELIA PHAM

MARI COPENY

ACTIVIST AND PHILANTHROPIST

When Mari was eight years old, crisis came to her hometown of Flint, Michigan. The city switched the source of its water supply and, suddenly, thousands of residents were exposed to unsafe chemicals in their drinking water. Instead of running clear, the water was a sludgy brown color.

Mari felt deeply connected to her community and wanted to do something to help. First she went to marches and joined protests and spoke out about the hardships her town was facing. But officials weren't acting fast enough, so Mari decided to try something new. She typed up a letter to someone she knew would be able to help: President Barack Obama. No one—not even Mari's mom!—thought the president was going to respond.

They were wrong. Not only did the president reply to Mari's letter, but he also flew to Flint to see what was going on. Soon after his trip, President Obama created a $100 million fund to go toward fixing the water crisis.

Mari didn't sit on the sidelines and watch the adults handle the situation—she raised hundreds of thousands of dollars herself so kids in her town could have access to free water bottles and school supplies. Later, she teamed up with a water filtration company to make her very own filter and donated it to any family in need.

Mari's age didn't stop her from making a difference in the world, and she continues to be an advocate today. "If they don't give you a seat at the table," Mari says, "stand on it with a megaphone."

BORN JULY 6, 2007
UNITED STATES OF AMERICA

"WE NEED TO PROTECT DREAMERS, WE NEED TO PROTECT KIDS IN THE MOST VULNERABLE AREAS, WE NEED LOVE AND FOR PEOPLE TO CARE ABOUT THEIR COMMUNITIES."
— MARI COPENY

4 YEARS FORGOTTEN

ILLUSTRATION BY
KITT THOMAS

MARIANA PAJÓN

BMX RIDER

When Mariana was growing up, her home city of Medellín, Colombia, was not a safe place. It was difficult to feel at peace when dangerous people were fighting in her city. But even when life was scary, Mariana was just like any other girl, dreaming exciting dreams and having fun with her family.

Mariana was three years old when she rode a bike for the first time. The wind whipped through her long hair, fanning it out like a cape. She felt so powerful as she pumped her legs, making her bike go faster and faster. Soon Mariana was competing in BMX races in her city. BMX racing is done on a dirt track with lots of hills and bumps. Few girls competed in BMX, but there was Mariana, winning race after race after race.

When she turned nine, Mariana entered her first international competition. As she waited at the starting line under the beating sun, Mariana was excited but also nervous. She was the only girl in the race. *What if I'm not as fast as boys?* she worried. Just then, the flag swung down and the race began. In an instant, Mariana swallowed her fear and took off. She pedaled as hard as she could. *Faster, faster!* she told herself.

She flew across the finish line. Her eyes widened as she heard the cheers and claps from the stands. She had won the race. After all the hardships she'd endured and seen at home, she was shocked. She'd become a world champion!

BORN OCTOBER 10, 1991
COLOMBIA

"WHATEVER HAPPENS, I KNOW I'LL ALWAYS ENJOY RACING."
—MARIANA PAJÓN

ILLUSTRATION BY ROCÍO CAPUTO

MARINE SERRE

FASHION DESIGNER

Before Marine Serre became a star on the runway, she was a star on the court. Growing up in France, Marine played tennis with hopes of going pro. She never imagined she would become a fashion designer or that sports would inspire her designs, but that's exactly what happened.

When Marine was a teenager, her interests turned toward art and clothes. She spent hours sifting through bins of colorful scarves and hand-me-down jeans in vintage shops. She started to mix and match unexpected pieces—like a delicate lace top with sporty leggings. Marine found inspiration for her personal style in everyday life. "I was looking at people in the street, my mom, my grandma, women I thought were beautiful," she said.

Marine went to fashion school and, in 2017, she became the youngest person to win the coveted LVMH Prize for Young Fashion Designers. The prize allowed her to debut her first collection at Paris Fashion Week. Cameras flashed as Marine's models strutted down the gleaming white runway wearing her designs. The clothes were athletic and playful, like a showstopping Lycra jumpsuit with a crescent moon print. Edgy and groundbreaking, Marine's clothes were made from recycled materials.

Marine's eco-friendly outfits quickly caught the attention of celebrities—Ariana Grande even wore the crescent moon jumpsuit on tour. Marine thinks everyone, from pop stars to everyday people, should keep one thing in mind when getting dressed: just have fun!

BORN DECEMBER 13, 1991

FRANCE

ILLUSTRATION BY
HAFSA SALOOJEE

"I THINK IT SHOULD
JUST BE NORMAL THAT
WE HAVE TO RECYCLE—
THAT'S THE WAY I WANT
TO ENGAGE PEOPLE."
—MARINE SERRE

MARITZA SOTO VÁSQUEZ

ASTRONOMER

Once upon a time in Chile, a child named Maritza fell in love with the night sky.

While other kids played outside after school, Maritza curled up in a chair and read her parents' encyclopedias. Before computers, these big, heavy books could tell her anything she wanted to know. It was like the whole world opened up to her in those pages!

Astronomy was the subject she liked best. She poured over her books, looking at the photos of planets, stars, and meteor showers. Later, she would gaze up and scan the velvety-black sky, looking for twinkling shapes in the night. Maritza imagined what it would be like to find a planet no one had ever seen before.

One day, when she was in graduate school, Maritza finally got her chance. For eight months, she'd been studying a solar system a lot like Earth's, with planets and stars and rocks hurtling through space. But she noticed something new. It was moving around a star in a circular path, just like the way Earth orbits around the sun. *What could that be?* she wondered. Peering through her telescope, she realized what she was seeing and gasped. She'd discovered a planet even bigger than Earth. It was even bigger than Jupiter. Imagine filling a bowl with 4,000 Earths—that's how big this planet was!

After years of reading about other astronomers' discoveries, Maritza had found a planet of her very own. She was excited to see what she would find the next time she looked up at the night sky.

BORN 1990

CHILE

ILLUSTRATION BY
GABY VERDOOREN

"NOBODY EVER TOLD ME
I COULD NOT DO IT . . .
BUT FEW WOMEN DARE."
—MARITZA SOTO VÁSQUEZ

MARLEY DIAS

ACTIVIST AND WRITER

I t was a crisp fall day in 2015, when a 10-year-old girl in New Jersey complained to her mom, saying: "All the books at school are about white boys and their dogs." Marley was frustrated with what teachers asked her to read. At home, her parents made sure her library was full of books with Black characters, but it was different in class.

"Well, what are you going to do about it?" asked her mom.

Marley had an idea. She launched the #1000BlackGirlBooks drive with the goal of collecting one thousand books with Black girl protagonists in a few months. As the drive was coming to an end, she'd only collected a few hundred. Time was running out. Marley's mom encouraged her to keep going. Marley was learning that sometimes being brave enough to do good things for your community took many tries. So she kept at it, and everything changed when the local news heard about her book drive.

The story went viral, and soon everyone wanted to hear about her big idea. Bloggers, schools, and millions of people around the world wanted to participate in the project. Marley collected more than 13,000 books.

Her life was becoming as exciting as the stories she devoured!

She spoke at the White House and published her own book. Next up, she began hosting a TV show called *Bookmarks: Celebrating Black Voices*. Marley's love of reading had inspired a movement.

Her advice for young girls? Use the things you care about as fuel to create positive change.

BORN JANUARY 3, 2005
UNITED STATES OF AMERICA

"BLACK GIRL STORIES AREN'T JUST FOR BLACK GIRLS. THEY'RE FOR EVERYBODY."
—MARLEY DIAS

ILLUSTRATION BY TAINA LAYLA CUNION

MEGAN JAYNE CRABBE

BODY POSITIVITY ADVOCATE

When Megan was growing up, she didn't like the way she looked. She wanted a smaller waist and a flat belly. She wanted perfect skin and long, flowing hair. Although Megan's family and friends told her she was beautiful, she didn't believe them. She didn't think she was beautiful at all.

One day, Megan realized why she felt this way. All around her, magazine articles, TV shows, movies, and social media posts were sending out a message. They were telling women everywhere that their bodies weren't good enough. Most of the time, these images weren't even real. The pictures had been altered. Megan was tired of letting these unrealistic images make her unhappy.

No more, Megan decided. *Someone has to make a change.*

So Megan started an Instagram account. In her photos, she didn't hide her real self. "You can be confident with acne and belly rolls," Megan reminded the world. "People of all sizes, shapes, shades, ages, genders, and abilities are beautiful."

Slowly, people began to listen to her. They shared their stories of insecurity and, like Megan, they joined the body positive revolution. In 2017, Megan wrote her first book. From there, she delivered talks, gave interviews, and hosted shows. She shouted her message for all to hear. Megan finally knew she was beautiful. She wanted others to realize they were too.

BORN JANUARY 20, 1993
UNITED KINGDOM

ILLUSTRATION BY
MICHELE MILLER

"IT DOESN'T REALLY
MATTER HOW YOU
LOOK IN PICTURES.
IT JUST MATTERS THAT
YOU'RE THERE."
—MEGAN JAYNE CRABBE

MIKAILA ULMER

ENTREPRENEUR

When Mikaila was four, she was stung by a bee *twice* in one week. Her ear swelled up like a tomato, and her neck ached. She was scared to go outside and play. To help conquer her fear, her parents encouraged her to learn about bees. Mikaila discovered that bees play an important role in the ecosystem and that they were dying off at an alarming rate.

Around the same time, Mikaila was trying to think of an idea for the local business competitions she'd entered. So far she had her interest in bees and a tattered cookbook from her great-grandma Helen that she'd just received in the mail. Gently, Mikaila turned page after page until she landed on a recipe for flaxseed lemonade. *Sweeten to taste*, it said. An idea buzzed into Mikaila's brain. How about a lemonade stand with homemade honey-sweetened lemonade!

Mikaila's newfound knowledge was the perfect icebreaker with her customers. *Did you know that bees have smelly feet?* she asked. She and her customers bonded over all kinds of bee facts, like how flowers and other plants can be fertilized by bees.

Those local competitions paved the way for Mikaila to go on a TV show for new business owners. After hearing her sweet pitch, an investor pledged $60,000 to help grow her business. Mikaila's brand, Me & the Bees Lemonade, now has five flavors and is sold in more than 1,800 stores. For every bottle she sells, she donates a portion of the profits to organizations that fight to save honeybees.

BORN SEPTEMBER 28, 2004
UNITED STATES OF AMERICA

"I KNOW THAT IF WE ALL GO OUT IN THIS WORLD LOOKING AT THE POSSIBILITIES OF THINGS INSTEAD OF JUST THE PROBLEMS, OUR FUTURE WILL BE A WHOLE LOT BRIGHTER."
—MIKAILA ULMER

ILLUSTRATION BY RONIQUE ELLIS

MILENA RADOYTSEVA

ANTI-BULLYING ACTIVIST

Once there was a girl who believed in kindness.

Milena was in a group chat online when she noticed people writing cruel comments to another kid. She didn't know how to stop it. "It started as a joke," she recalled. "I just sat and watched."

Never again, she promised.

Milena became interested in anti-bullying activism. She knew that bullies often have struggles of their own. So she decided to use compassion to reach out to kids who take out their frustrations on other kids over the internet.

Milena joined a youth panel called the Safer Internet Center, or SafeNet. She knew she was a strong communicator. In addition to her native Bulgarian, she spoke English and German. Milena used her language and storytelling skills to help her team at SafeNet come up with campaigns to reach out to online bullies. In one video, a cyberbully sees his little sister draw a picture of him as a superhero. When he realizes he hasn't been acting like a hero at all, he decides to change the way he deals with his anger.

Milena knows she's fighting an uphill battle. "The internet will never be this totally happy place with rainbows," she said. But she believes it can be made a lot safer for young people.

At conferences, in videos, and through interviews, Milena spreads her message of understanding. "I want to speak about things that need to be spoken about," she's said. She knows she'll never stay silent again.

BORN JANUARY 8, 2004
BULGARIA

ILLUSTRATION BY
PHOEBE FALCONER

"EVERYONE IS A HERO INSIDE,
BUT IT IS A QUESTION OF
FINDING ONE'S ESSENCE."
—MILENA RADOYTSEVA

MILLIE BOBBY BROWN

ACTOR AND CHILDREN'S RIGHTS ADVOCATE

Once upon a time, a girl named Millie found her calling in front of the TV. She was drawn to romantic movies and musicals and spent hours memorizing lines from her favorite scenes to train herself to act and sing. One of her idols was the famous actor, Audrey Hepburn. Millie looked up to her because of her talent and her charity work helping kids around the world.

Millie was determined to make her dream come true even when others tried to break her spirit. In school, she was bullied by a group of students. It got so bad that eventually she decided to switch schools.

With the support of her family, Millie continued to pursue acting. "Once I find something I want to do, nobody's stopping me," she said. Millie went on countless auditions. She kept telling herself, *One day, I'll make it*. And then, at age 11, she got her first big break, playing Eleven, a troubled girl with supernatural powers, in a show called *Stranger Things*. While auditioning, her strong-willed nature gave her an edge. She invented her character's signature glare—eyes narrowed, brows slanted into a razor-sharp V, chin tucked—on the spot. It's the look that instantly spooks anyone who dares to cross Eleven.

After bringing Eleven to life, Millie landed another dream role as UNICEF's youngest-ever goodwill ambassador. Just like Audrey Hepburn, Millie travels the world speaking up for children who suffer from bullying, violence, and poverty. By remaining true to herself, Millie has gone from looking up to the stars to being one.

BORN FEBRUARY 19, 2004
UNITED KINGDOM

"YOUNG PEOPLE DON'T WANT TO BE TALKED ABOUT. WE WANT TO DO THE TALKING."
—MILLIE BOBBY BROWN

ILLUSTRATION BY
MARELLA MOON ALBANESE

MO'NE DAVIS

On a cloudy Friday afternoon at the Little League World Series, Mo'ne stepped onto the pitcher's mound. Her long braids, tied back in a low ponytail, swung to her waist. She adjusted her maroon cap, took a deep breath, and threw the ball, putting all her strength in the pitch. The batter froze. Strike one. Mo'ne set up again and threw another fastball. Strike two. She threw another. Strike three. The next batter struck out too. And the one after him.

In six innings, Mo'ne struck out eight batters to become the first girl in Little League World Series history to pitch a shutout. Her 70-mile-an-hour fastball was unstoppable! Overnight, it seemed like everyone knew her name. She appeared on the cover of *Sports Illustrated* and won an award for being the best breakthrough athlete. President Obama even invited her to the White House.

But before all the praise and kind words, there were a lot of people who didn't believe in Mo'ne. The first time she walked onto the field for a Little League game, she heard the boys on the other team making fun of her. It was going to be an easy win, they said, because she was a girl. Even the grown-ups were laughing. Mo'ne didn't say anything—she let her pitching do the talking. "When they saw me face the first batter, they were shocked," she said.

Mo'ne's belief in herself—and her spectacular fastball—took her team all the way to the Little League World Series. She made baseball history and reminded everyone of the true power of "throwing like a girl."

BORN JUNE 24, 2001
UNITED STATES OF AMERICA

"JUST BECAUSE I'M A GIRL DOESN'T MEAN ANYTHING. I KEPT GETTING BETTER, AND THE GAME GOT BETTER."
—MO'NE DAVIS

ILLUSTRATION BY TONI D. CHAMBERS

MOMOKO NOJO

ACTIVIST

When Momoko first heard that Japan was going to host the 2020 Olympics in Tokyo, she was excited. She knew this giant, international event would go down in history. But when a 70-something-year-old man was chosen as president of the Olympic Organizing Committee, Momoko was disappointed. *Important positions like this always go to older men,* she lamented. *Young people, especially young women, are often ignored by the government.*

Before the Olympics were underway, the newly appointed president said something awful and sexist: *When women are in meetings, the meetings never end, because women talk too much.*

Momoko could not believe her ears.

She rushed to her computer and started a social media campaign using the hashtag #DontBeSilent. She also wrote up a petition calling for action against the committee president—and in less than two weeks, 150,000 people signed it. Clearly Momoko was not the only one who knew how wrong the president's statement was. Her petition and the #DontBeSilent campaign pressured him to resign from his position.

Momoko was ecstatic! She was even more thrilled when she learned his role would be filled by a woman, an athlete who had competed in seven Olympic games.

"If you raise your voice and get the support you need, you can definitely make a difference," she said. Momoko plans to keep standing up against things she knows are wrong. And she wants all the young people in Japan to join her.

BORN MARCH 17, 1998

JAPAN

"I DON'T WANT OUR NEXT GENERATION TO SPEND THEIR TIME OVER THIS ISSUE."
—MOMOKO NOJO

ILLUSTRATION BY YIYI CHEN

MONTANNAH KENNEY

MOUNTAIN CLIMBER

Montannah and her mom were always an excellent team. Their bond became even stronger when, at seven years old, Montannah proposed a grand feat: to climb to the top of Mount Kilimanjaro, the tallest mountain in Africa. The idea of going on an adventure with her mom was thrilling, but she had another idea too. She explained, "I wanted to be closer to my dad." Montannah's dad passed away when she was three. She said she felt him watching over her.

Montannah knew the climb would be a challenge. She trained for months. Her mom had to secure a special permit for Montannah and hire a team to accompany them and keep them safe.

Finally, the first day of the climb arrived. Montannah, her mom, and their guides bundled up and started up the mountain. For more than a week, they scrambled over rocks and hiked through rain, fog, and snow. Sometimes Montannah couldn't tell what was a cliff and what was a cloud. But she made it to the top. Standing on the peak of the mountain, with the cold wind whistling, Montannah felt happy and proud. She had broken a world record and was the youngest girl to reach the top of Kilimanjaro! She blew kisses into the sky for her dad to catch.

Montannah's historic hike wasn't just a hike. She and her mom used it to raise money for EMDR, a type of therapy for patients with post-traumatic stress disorder, or PTSD. Montannah's father was going through the same treatment before he died. Montannah wanted to make it possible for other people to complete their own grand feats.

BORN MAY 2010
UNITED STATES OF AMERICA

"I BLEW KISSES TO MY DAD, SO HE KNEW I WAS THERE." —MONTANNAH KENNEY

ILLUSTRATION BY ZUZA KAMIŃSKA

NALLELI COBO

ENVIRONMENTAL ACTIVIST

Nalleli was nine years old when she started noticing a strange stench wafting through her neighborhood streets. It smelled like guava. Soon Nalleli was sick, and so were many other people in her community.

When she asked her mother why so many people were unwell, Nalleli learned that it was because of their neighbor across the street—an enormous oil well. The site was drilling more than ever. And it was using the guava scent to mask the poisonous toxins polluting the air. *How could this be happening in the middle of Los Angeles?* She needed to know.

Nalleli and her mom teamed up to unite their community against the oil company. They went door to door to rally their neighbors as part of their campaign, People Not Pozos. (*Pozos* refers to oil wells in Spanish.)

Even though Nalleli was young, she spoke at town and city hall meetings on her neighborhood's behalf. When she was 13, she even appealed to the pope! All over the country, people and politicians took notice. Finally, after all her hard work, Nalleli got the phone call she'd been waiting for: the oil drilling site in her neighborhood was closing and the air would become safe to breathe again.

Nalleli knows she must remain alert. She works with Stand Together Against Neighborhood Drilling (STAND-LA), and she has cofounded an organization called the South Central Youth Leadership Coalition. She says that for her, "environmental justice is being able to breathe clean air regardless of my age, gender, race, socioeconomic status, or ZIP code."

BORN DECEMBER 19, 2000
UNITED STATES OF AMERICA

"WE WON, AND IT WAS TEN TIMES MORE AWESOME BECAUSE IT WAS THE YOUTH DEMANDING OUR RIGHT TO A LIVABLE FUTURE."
—NALLELI COBO

ILLUSTRATION BY SARA CANSINO

NAOMI WADLER

ACTIVIST

Once upon a time, a girl went from watching the news to making the news. As Naomi did homework and chores, her parents always played the news on TV in the background. In 2018, when the story broke about a shooting at a high school in Parkland, Florida, she looked on, feeling angry and scared. Naomi also watched as young people in high schools and middle schools across the United States protested gun violence. Then she vowed she would do more than just watch.

Naomi and her best friend brainstormed ideas on how to use their voices. They decided to organize a protest in the form of a walkout. One day, she and 60 of her classmates got up from their desks and marched out of school. They stood together in silence to honor victims of gun violence. Naomi's protest caught the attention of a national movement. The organizer of the March for Our Lives protest in Washington, DC, contacted her to address the enormous crowd.

Naomi spoke from her heart about how gun violence impacts everyone in the country, even if some stories don't get equal attention. "I am here today to acknowledge and represent the African American girls whose stories don't make the front page of every national newspaper," she said. Naomi wasn't expecting to get the response she did. She heard the cheers from the crowd and knew she'd inspired thousands more watching her at home. The little girl who was so used to simply watching was now the one doing.

BORN OCTOBER 16, 2006
ETHIOPIA AND UNITED STATES OF AMERICA

ILLUSTRATION BY
NOA DENMON

"ONCE WE RESPECT OURSELVES, WE
CAN TREAT OUR BODIES AND OUR
MINDS WITH LOVE . . . THAT IS WHEN
OUR MAGIC IS AT ITS MOST POWERFUL."
—NAOMI WADLER

NORA AL MATROOSHI

ASTRONAUT

Nora's dream of becoming an astronaut began in kindergarten. One day, her teacher handed out arts-and-crafts supplies and told the class to make helmets and backpacks for their mission to the moon. Then Nora's teacher pitched a tent in the middle of the classroom. The tent would be their spaceship.

The students crawled inside. Nora squeezed her eyes shut. She could almost feel the rumbling of their pretend spaceship as it blasted off. Nora had lived in the United Arab Emirates her whole life—she had never been to the moon before! What was it going to be like?

When Nora burst out of the tent, her classroom had been completely transformed. It was pitch-black and everything was covered in pieces of gray cloth to represent the moon's rocky surface. Nora was hooked. She knew that when she grew up she was going to go to the *real* moon.

After studying mechanical engineering in college, Nora's astronaut training got underway. It was full of tests—both physical and mental. As part of her training, Nora was interviewed by a panel of astronauts, including two astronauts from her home country and two female astronauts. It was both nerve-wracking and exciting to have a chance to talk to the very people Nora admired.

When Nora got the news that she was selected to be an astronaut, she was overjoyed. She would be the first Arab woman astronaut ever! Nora was well on her way to accomplishing the goal she set for herself that day in kindergarten: to step foot on the *real* moon.

DISCOVER MORE

BORN CIRCA 1993
UNITED ARAB EMIRATES

ILLUSTRATION BY
MALIHA ABIDI

"IF YOU CAN'T FIND
[OPPORTUNITIES], THEN
CREATE THEM FOR YOURSELF."
—NORA AL MATROOSHI

PUISAND LAI

Puisand had always dreamed of being an athlete. As a little girl, she was constantly on the move—running and racing and jumping all around.

When Puisand was six years old, she received life-changing news. She was diagnosed with a rare nerve condition. Puisand had to start using a wheelchair, and many people thought her athletic dreams were dashed. But there was no way she was quitting.

When she was 13, Puisand joined a wheelchair tennis program. She wanted to make friends and learn the game. Shocked and proud, she found out she was more talented than she'd realized. She could hit the tennis ball with a powerful *whack!* and race across the court faster than anyone else.

A year later, Puisand set off to a tennis camp for people using wheelchairs. She practiced her pivots, swings, and serves. By 2017, she was listed as seventh in the International Tennis Federation rankings for girls' wheelchair tennis. But was one sport enough? Not for Puisand! She set her sights on becoming an all-round sports superstar.

When Puisand started wheelchair basketball, she picked it up quickly and was soon recruited to join Team Ontario. She won gold at the 2017 Ontario Winter Games and competed at the 2018 Wheelchair Basketball World Championship as part of the Canadian national team. Then, in 2021, one of Puisand's biggest dreams came true—she competed in the Paralympic Games in Tokyo.

BORN JULY 29, 2000

CANADA

ILLUSTRATION BY
VIVIENNE SHAO

"BASKETBALL HAS DEFINITELY
GIVEN ME THE CHANCE TO SEE
THE WORLD AND TRAVEL TO ALL
OF THESE DIFFERENT PLACES THAT
I DIDN'T KNOW A LOT ABOUT."
—PUISAND LAI

QUAN HONGCHAN

DIVER

Hongchan grew up in a small village in Guangdong, China, where her parents worked as farmers. They didn't make much money, so Hongchan and her four siblings never got to visit exciting places like amusement parks or zoos.

One day, she was playing a game of hopscotch with her friends. A former diver and coach from a sports school noticed something special about her. She had such a small frame, but she could jump long distances, like a graceful snow leopard. He asked Hongchan's parents if he could train her as a diver.

Hongchan spent years perfecting her pikes, tucks, and twists, and when she was 14, she went to the Olympics. At the time, her mom was sick, and Hongchan knew her performance would mean a lot to her family. The crowd watched the tiny girl walk up to the 10-meter platform (that's as tall as a school bus is long!). Hongchan calmly placed her hands on the platform and raised her legs into the air. From her handstand, she launched into the air, somersaulted twice, and twisted one and a half times before plunging into the water. The crowd roared! Her next four dives were as impressive as her first, earning her two perfect 10s. Hongchan was the youngest gold medalist at the Tokyo Olympics.

Everyone in China was proud of her, and the hospital gave her mother free treatment. To honor their champion, an amusement park in Guangdong decided to give free memberships to all divers on the Chinese team. Hongchan could not wait to dive in!

BORN MARCH 28, 2007
CHINA

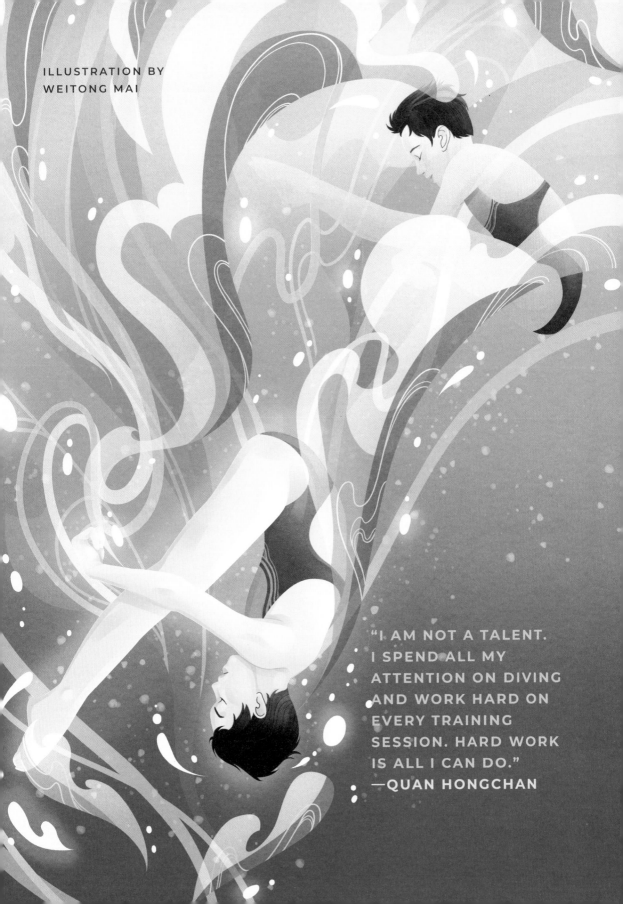

ILLUSTRATION BY
WEITONG MAI

"I AM NOT A TALENT.
I SPEND ALL MY
ATTENTION ON DIVING
AND WORK HARD ON
EVERY TRAINING
SESSION. HARD WORK
IS ALL I CAN DO."
—QUAN HONGCHAN

RAYOUF ALHUMEDHI

ACTIVIST AND PRODUCT DESIGNER

Rayouf had friends in different parts of the world. Before moving to Germany, she'd lived in Saudi Arabia with her family. She texted her friends in both countries all the time—about school, news, and their hopes and dreams for the future.

One day, she and a few of her friends were creating a new group chat. Rayouf realized that everyone had an emoji that looked like them— except for her. As a Muslim girl, she wore a hijab that covered her hair and neck as a sign of her faith. She had hijabs in all different colors and materials. But there wasn't a single emoji on her phone with a hijab.

This is baffling, thought Rayouf. *Why isn't there an emoji to represent me and the millions of other hijabi women across the world?*

It just didn't make sense.

Rayouf kept thinking about it. She didn't always like how she was treated when she wore a hijab in public. And she was often bothered by how girls like her appeared in film and television. *Maybe*, thought Rayouf, *people just need to see us more often*.

She designed a hijabi emoji and wrote an explanation for why it was important. Rayouf then presented her idea in front of major computer and tech companies. Her simple, clever idea caught fire. Soon she was fielding calls from newspapers in between her high school classes. About a year after she shared her proposal, the emoji was released. Now when Rayouf is in group chats, she can choose an emoji that looks just like her—one that she created!

BORN MARCH 30, 2001
SAUDI ARABIA AND GERMANY

ILLUSTRATION BY
MAEDEH MOSAVERZADEH

"REPRESENTATION IS A
CAUSE I WILL ALWAYS
STAND FOR."
—RAYOUF ALHUMEDHI

RAYSSA LEAL

SKATEBOARDER

Once upon a time in Brazil, there was a little girl named Rayssa whose love for skateboarding took her to great heights.

In the skate parks Rayssa went to, she saw only boys skating. But that was okay. She was happiest when she was zipping through the world on nothing but a board and four wheels. She soared down half-pipes, slid along handrails, and learned all the tricks and jumps she could. To Rayssa, skateboarding felt like flying.

What if I could really fly? Rayssa wondered.

So one day when she was seven, she decided to dress up in a bright blue fairy princess costume, complete with a pair of wings. The outfit made her invincible. It was the perfect way to learn one of the most difficult skateboarding tricks: the heel flip.

Skating toward the top of a staircase, Rayssa needed to launch herself into the air with enough power to flip her board beneath her feet. Then she'd land back on her board at the bottom of the steps. With a friend there to film her, she tried and tried but couldn't stick the landing.

Rayssa was about to give up and go home. Then she decided to try one last time. She knew she could do it. This time, she jumped higher than she ever had. As she lifted her knees, her skateboard spun beneath her. She cleared the stairs and landed perfectly on her board. Rayssa beamed as her friends erupted in cheers. Thousands of people watched her video online. Just a few years later, Rayssa flew all the way to Tokyo and became Brazil's youngest ever Olympic medalist!

BORN JANUARY 4, 2008
BRAZIL

"I WANT OTHER GIRLS TO HAVE THE SAME OPPORTUNITY AS ME TO SEE THEIR LIVES AND DREAMS COME TRUE THROUGH SPORTS."
—RAYSSA LEAL

ILLUSTRATION BY PAULA ZORITE

REBECCA ROOS JENSEN

PILOT

As a child, Rebecca was terrified of flying. Sitting in her seat on an airplane, her palms would sweat, and she'd feel like she was going to throw up. Traveling out of Denmark to vacation with her family was so much fun, but she dreaded the plane trip every time. It seemed completely impossible to her that a giant metal box could stay high up in the air for hundreds of miles.

At 16 years old, Rebecca decided to conquer her fear. If she was afraid of being an airplane passenger, she thought, maybe she would have better luck as a pilot. "I have always liked to take control of things myself," she said.

She took flight lessons and studied flight theory every night. Then the day came for her to climb into the cockpit of a two-person plane for the first time. The runway was long and intimidating. But Rebecca had done her homework. She took a deep breath. "Ready to taxi," she said into the radio. The plane glided down the runway, zooming faster and faster, until it was just fast enough to take off. Up Rebecca went! *So this is what it is like to fly*, Rebecca thought. *What a wonderful feeling!* She watched houses and trees grow smaller and smaller beneath her.

Forty-five hours of flying lessons and one pilot test later, Rebecca was handed what she'd worked so hard for: her very own private pilot license. With it, she'd become the youngest female pilot in Denmark. After years of being terrified of flying, it's now Rebecca's greatest joy. "There are just some things one has to overcome," she says.

BORN AUGUST 19, 2001

DENMARK

"WHEN YOU FLY, IT REQUIRES
FULL CONCENTRATION, AND
THEREFORE YOU FORGET ALL THE
THINGS FROM EVERYDAY LIFE."
—REBECCA ROOS JENSEN

RENATA FLORES

SINGER-SONGWRITER

Once upon a time in Ayacucho, Peru, there lived a girl named Renata. Surrounded by soaring mountains that touched the clouds, Ayacucho was filled with the ancient ruins of the Indigenous tribes who had lived there for thousands of years. Renata grew up immersed in history, listening to her grandparents chat in a language she couldn't understand.

The language was known as Quechua, or Runasimi. Lots of other Indigenous families in her area knew it, but young people weren't taught it. Renata felt connected to her heritage and wanted to preserve the language, so she decided to learn Quechua.

Renata's grandmothers pitched in, showing her how to pronounce words correctly. She also enrolled in language classes, to help her speak with confidence. Soon she wasn't just speaking in Quechua, she was singing! And she had a wonderful idea: maybe the way to preserve her ancestors' language was through music.

When she was 14 years old, she filmed herself singing "The Way You Make Me Feel" by Michael Jackson. But in her version, the lyrics were all in Quechua. Millions of people watched the video, entranced by Renata's singing voice. Many were inspired to relearn—and be proud of—the languages their families had lost.

Renata now releases her own original songs. Like a lyrical bridge from the past to the future, she sings about Indigenous rights and the revolutionary Quechua women who have come before her.

BORN MARCH 20, 2001

PERU

"THERE ARE OTHER INDIGENOUS LANGUAGES WE MUST SAVE TOO. I FEEL LIKE WE ARE STILL GETTING TO KNOW OURSELVES AND ACCEPTING OURSELVES. WE MUST BE PROUD AND TAKE ACTION." —RENATA FLORES

ILLUSTRATION BY TAMIKI

RESHMA KOSARAJU

COMPUTER SCIENTIST AND INVENTOR

Reshma was tired—tired of living with the effects of wildfires in her home state of California. The smoke stung her eyes and lingered in her hair. It was difficult to breathe, so she couldn't play outside freely. Still, Reshma knew she was lucky. Lots of people had to evacuate. Some even lost their homes.

She wanted to help find a solution. She had heard of something called an artificial intelligence, or AI, model, that people program on their computers to predict things, like the weather. That gave her an idea. "I wanted to investigate and see if I could figure out a way to predict fires before they occurred, which could save lives, money, and the environment," Reshma said.

There was only one problem: Reshma didn't know how to create an AI model. *Well,* she thought, *I guess I have a lot to learn!*

Reshma spent three years studying AI. Then she studied all the things that might start a fire. Is the area humid or windy? Is the soil too dry? Are there lots of people camping nearby?

She taught her computer to consider all of these variables. When she was done, her program could tell when and where forest fires might start. Reshma won the Children's Climate Prize for her model.

Next Reshma wants to make an app that will alert people if a fire is getting close. That way, firefighters will have a better chance of keeping flames under control, and kids across the country will know when it is safe to play outside in the fresh air.

BORN CIRCA 2006
UNITED STATES OF AMERICA

"THIS VALIDATION FROM THE SCIENTIFIC COMMUNITY AND THE PUBLIC AT LARGE HAS GIVEN ME THE CONFIDENCE I NEED TO CONTINUE DOING WHAT I AM DOING."
—RESHMA KOSARAJU

ILLUSTRATION BY AVANI DWIVEDI

RIYA KARUMANCHI

INVENTOR AND ENTREPRENEUR

Riya was visiting a friend's house when she noticed that her friend's grandmother kept bumping into things. She had a visual impairment, and the white cane she used when she walked around hadn't been updated in a century. It was just a stick! *Don't my friend's grandmother—and all visually impaired people—deserve to benefit from advances in technology and design?* she thought.

Riya decided that it was about time someone made a smarter cane. For a school science fair project, Riya and a friend worked on a prototype of a cane with a sensor that would allow visually impaired people to "see" objects above the knee. Their SmartCane won first prize!

But for Riya, SmartCane wasn't just a project for a science fair. She kept working on it, bringing it to hackathons, where she learned to code and develop the technology in the cane further. She added new features, like a GPS that vibrated to give SmartCane users directions: one buzz for left, two buzzes for right. Riya even studied business so she could turn SmartCane into a real product, available on the market. Big tech companies were so impressed with her work and creativity that they invested tens of thousands of dollars in her business.

What was it like to be a young inventor? reporters asked Riya. "We're living in one of the best times in history to create things and pursue our passions," she replied. "And there are more resources than ever before to help you." Nothing should stop kids from working on their big ideas. "The worst that can happen is you learn," said Riya with a twinkle in her eye.

BORN CIRCA 2003
CANADA

"PEOPLE MAY NOT ALWAYS LIKE YOUR IDEA, AND YOU HAVE TO WORK HARD FOR IT AND PUT IN THE EFFORT AND TIME. THAT'S WHAT WILL GET YOU PLACES."
—RIYA KARUMANCHI

ILLUSTRATION BY AVANI DWIVEDI

ROBABA MOHAMMADI

PAINTER

Once upon a time, there was a girl who defied expectations. Robaba dreamed of being an artist, but many people thought she would not be able to paint because she was born with a disability. Her hands and feet were paralyzed, so she couldn't move them. Still, she believed that she was capable of achieving her goal.

Since Robaba couldn't hold a pencil with her hand, her father encouraged her to try holding it in her mouth. It was tricky at first, but she kept at it. First, she perfected drawing a straight line, then she moved on to more complex shapes. A friend gave Robaba an art book, and she learned techniques like shading and perspective. She began to paint and draw lifelike portraits of people. "I do paintings mostly about Afghan women, women's power, the beauty of women," Robaba said. In a few years, she created 200 pieces of art!

She was proud of her work and wanted to share the joy of creativity with others. So she began giving painting lessons in her home. Everyone was welcome at Robaba's classes.

Word of her art classes spread, and soon, Robaba was able to open her own arts center. She teaches students of all abilities how to create their own masterpieces. In the future, she hopes to expand her center to include literacy classes for people with disabilities.

Robaba knows that Afghan girls face serious challenges and that girls with disabilites face tougher situations still. She's achieved her goal and will keep fighting so other girls can reach their goals too.

BORN SEPTEMBER 30, 2000
AFGHANISTAN

"I WANT TO EXPRESS MY DREAMS, MY FEELINGS, AND MY WORLD THROUGH MY PAINTING."
—ROBABA MOHAMMADI

ILLUSTRATION BY
ZAHRA SOLTANIAN
(SHIISSO)

RUBY KATE CHITSEY

PHILANTHROPIST

Once upon a time, a 10-year-old girl became a fairy godmother. But instead of a wand and fairy dust, Ruby Kate used a simple notebook and her can-do spirit to bring people joy.

Ruby Kate's mom is a nurse, so Ruby Kate grew up volunteering in assisted living homes. One day, while helping her mom at one of the homes, she noticed a resident named Pearl gazing out her window, looking upset. Pearl could not take her dog with her. She didn't know when she would see her beloved pet again.

"Why?" asked Ruby Kate. Pearl explained that it cost money to have someone care for the dog and bring her on visits—she couldn't afford it.

Pearl's story broke Ruby Kate's heart. After talking to some of the other residents, she heard other similar stories. Many people in nursing homes did not have access to the things they once enjoyed. So Ruby Kate took action. She got out her notebook and asked the residents for their three wishes. Wishes included things like new clothes, chocolate treats, and of course, supplies for furry friends. With the support of her community, Ruby Kate began granting residents' wishes—and that's how she earned the title of fairy godmother.

Ruby Kate founded an organization, Three Wishes for Ruby's Residents, and has since granted more than 25,000 wishes. By 14 years old, she had expanded her program to include a team of young people who help her make wishes come true. Volunteering is her favorite thing to do, and she encourages others to follow in her footsteps.

BORN OCTOBER 11, 2007
UNITED STATES OF AMERICA

"I STARTED SMALL AND WORKED HARD TO ACHIEVE MY GOAL. I HAVE GRIT."
—RUBY KATE CHITSEY

ILLUSTRATION BY JIALEI SUN

SADIQUA BYNUM

GYMNAST AND STUNTWOMAN

Once upon a time, a two-year-old girl learned to do the cartwheels that would eventually land her in Hollywood. Under the fluorescent lights, Sadiqua perfected flipping on the mat, leaping on the balance beam, and swinging on the uneven bars. By the time she turned 15, she was coaching other kids.

In college at UCLA, Sadiqua performed floor routines to pop songs with a bright smile and chalky feet. Crowds clapped to the beat and watched in anticipation of what she would do next. Her blue uniform sparkled as she sprang off the ground and soared through the air. When she graduated, the nationally ranked gymnast was a three-time All-American—a title reserved only for top gymnasts.

But Sadiqua's most daring leap of faith was becoming one of Hollywood's youngest stuntwomen. When a character in a movie has to do an exhilarating action scene, sometimes a stuntperson takes over. And sometimes that person is Sadiqua. She might ride horses or motorcycles or perform fast-paced fight scenes where her killer gymnastics skills are on full display.

It's not as easy as she makes it look on the big screen. "Sometimes there's glitz," Sadiqua says. "And sometimes there are bruises and scrapes and cuts." Still she finds it thrilling. One day, she hopes to learn to drive planes and boats. Whether it's in the sky, on the water, or in a gym, Sadiqua can be found flipping into the action, just as she did when she was a toddler.

BORN NOVEMBER 18, 1993
UNITED STATES OF AMERICA

"IT'S IMPORTANT FOR BLACK WOMEN TO SHOW OUR OWN POWER."
—SADIQUA BYNUM

ILLUSTRATION BY
TAINA LAYLA CUNION

SAPANA

NURSE

There once was a girl who daydreamed of healing people with rays of light from her hands. Her name was Sapana, and when she was a girl, her younger sister fell ill. Her family lived far from a hospital, so they performed a traditional healing ceremony to try and cure her. Sapana begged her father to make the journey to a medical clinic, but by the time they set off through the jungle, it was too late, and her sister died. At that moment, Sapana promised herself she would become a nurse.

Every day, she walked for four hours to get to school. And when monsoons flooded the roads, she slept overnight in her classroom. Finally, the day came for her to apply to nursing school and take the entrance exam. Sadly, Sapana was not accepted. She remembered the advice of a mentor from when she was younger, who told her to never underestimate herself. "I realized I had the strength to keep trying," Sapana said. "I was not going to stop there."

She prepared for months and retook the exam. When the results were posted, she stood at the window and scanned through the list of names of students who had passed. There, in the middle of the list, in big, black, all-capital letters, she saw her name: SAPANA!

As a nurse, Sapana is inspired by Florence Nightingale. "When my sister was sick, I felt helpless, and I wished I was Florence. I wanted to know what gave her the strength to keep working for others."

Many might wonder the same about Sapana.

BORN 1994

NEPAL

"SOMETIMES ALL YOU CAN DO IS NOT GIVE UP!"
—SAPANA

ILLUSTRATION BY BANDANA TULACHAN

SARAH VOSS

GYMNAST

Sarah was five years old when her mom enrolled her in her first tumbling class. Since that fateful day, Sarah's entire future was dedicated to gymnastics. Inspired by athletes like Nastia Liukin, Shawn Johnson, and Simone Biles, she trained up to 30 hours a week, perfecting her handsprings, layouts, and splits.

But as Sarah got older and her body began to change, she started to feel less comfortable in the traditional bikini cut leotards most gymnasts wear. So she decided to make a change.

Sarah slipped on a full bodysuit and headed to a meet. With her arms and legs covered, she was the first gymnast to wear a bodysuit at a major international competition without a religious reason. Her new style made her more comfortable performing. And Sarah had another reason for her costume change—to encourage girls everywhere to stick with gymnastics. She realized that many young athletes quit the sport when they go through puberty. Full body leotards could help them feel more secure as they land their front flips and nail their round-offs. "This is a great option for everyone to stay in the sport they love," she said.

Sarah's teammates followed suit, and together they bounded onto the mats at the 2020 Olympics wearing matching sparkly, leg-covering one-pieces. "We hope gymnasts uncomfortable in the usual outfits will feel emboldened to follow our example," Sarah said. Without having to worry about what she's wearing, Sarah can get back to doing what she does best: gymnastics!

BORN OCTOBER 21, 1999
GERMANY

ILLUSTRATION BY SIBEL BALAC

VOSS

"FEELING GOOD
AND STILL LOOKING
ELEGANT? WHY NOT?"
—SARAH VOSS

SHAINE KILYUN

PET WHEELCHAIR MAKER

Shaine loved all creatures, big and small. She knew she wanted to dedicate her life to animals—big fluffy dogs, tiny mice, great-winged birds—but how? *Maybe I could become a vet,* she pondered, *and take care of animals that are sick or injured. Or maybe I could open a rescue shelter for animals without homes.*

One day, Shaine was surfing the web when she came across a video tutorial on how to make a wheelchair for a dog. *What a creative way to do something for animals in need!* Shaine thought. She was a little worried that no one would want to trust their dog to a wheelchair made by a 15-year-old, but she had to give it a try.

Shaine purchased plastic piping and the other supplies she needed to make her first doggie wheelchair and got to work. She started an Instagram account for her new project called Wheelies and shared photos of her wheelchairs as they grew more sophisticated. After a few months, she was receiving requests from around the world.

She's made large, sturdy wheelchairs for labradors, and tiny, lightweight wheelchairs for chihuahuas. She's built wheelchairs for cats, a hedgehog, and even a duck!

Her Wheelies have made it possible for animals who might never be adopted to find loving homes. She donates many of her creations to animal shelters, rescues, and sanctuaries.

"I truly want to make a difference for as many animals as I possibly can," Shaine says.

BORN SEPTEMBER 16, 2005
UNITED STATES OF AMERICA

"YOU CAN MAKE A DIFFERENCE
NO MATTER WHAT YOUR AGE IS."
—SHAINE KILYUN

ILLUSTRATION BY
MELISA FERNÁNDEZ NITSCHE

SHIRA STRONGIN

DISABILITY RIGHTS ADVOCATE

Shira never wanted to stand out in middle school. But it was hard to fly below the radar when she would disappear from class for a few weeks and then appear again in a wheelchair. When one of her classmates called her a "sick chick," she was hurt and angry. She didn't want to tell him about the seizures she'd been having. They were none of his business! But Shira knew that most kids her age didn't understand anything about disability or chronic illness, especially an illness like hers.

Shira has a progressive neurovascular disease. She was very sick, yet no doctor could figure out what was causing her symptoms, so they didn't know how to treat it. Even if no one could understand what was happening to her body, Shira thought that maybe she could educate them about her experience.

Under the pen name Sick Chick, Shira started a blog. She wrote about being in and out of the hospital. She wrote about her surgeries and the interactions she had with kids at school. One day, a nonprofit organization reached out to Shira and asked her to speak at an event. Suddenly she realized she was doing something really important. There were girls like her all over the world—sick chicks who needed to see and hear their stories told. And these young people needed to find one another. She built Sick Chicks into a global network of young women, brought together to form a safe space and take action on behalf of all people living with illness and disability. Shira realized she might be a sick chick, but she could still get a whole lot done.

BORN MARCH 29, 1999
UNITED STATES OF AMERICA

ILLUSTRATION BY
SANNA LEGAN

"SOME OF THE MOST PASSIONATE
ADVOCATES I HAVE MET HAVE
BEEN YOUNG—BECAUSE WE'RE
FIGHTING FOR OUR FUTURE."
—SHIRA STRONGIN

SIFAN HASSAN

LONG-DISTANCE RUNNER

Sifan was an incredible runner. In fact, her stride was so strong and her pace was so quick that she took her talents to meets all around the world. But it was while she was competing in the Tokyo Olympics in 2021, that a runner's greatest fear came to pass for her.

Sifan was entering the last lap of the women's 1,500-meter preliminary race—a race that would determine who would qualify for the final round—when a runner ahead of her tripped. She tried to jump over the fallen runner but ended up falling herself. In an instant, sure-footed Sifan was in second to last place.

That wasn't the end of the race for her. Sifan sprang to her feet with a new challenge to overcome. Her feet pounded the track as she pumped her arms and pushed her legs. She used all her energy and determination to keep going. One by one, she sped by the other runners until she flew past the finish line—in first place!

Later that same day, she competed in the women's 5,000-meter race, earning herself a gold medal. A few days after that, she secured a bronze medal in the 1,500-meter race and another gold medal in the 10,000-meter race.

Sifan became the first Dutch woman to win a medal in a long-distance race and the first athlete in history to win medals in the 1,500-meter, 5,000-meter, and 10,000-meter events at a single Olympic Games. Her tenacity is proof that even when a person falls, she can get back up, become stronger than ever, and maybe even win a medal . . . or three.

BORN JANUARY 1, 1993
THE NETHERLANDS

"FOR ME, IT IS CRUCIAL TO FOLLOW MY HEART. DOING THAT IS FAR MORE IMPORTANT THAN GOLD MEDALS."
—SIFAN HASSAN

ILLUSTRATION BY NAKI NARH

SOPHIE CRUZ

IMMIGRATION ACTIVIST

Once there was a girl who loved her family more than anything. But Sophie lived in fear that her family would be torn apart. Her parents were undocumented immigrants living in the United States. The Cruzes had left Oaxaca, Mexico, and moved to California for a better life. Being undocumented made things very difficult for Sophie's parents. They lived with the constant threat of deportation—being forced to leave their home and return to Mexico. Sophie felt it wasn't fair that her family had to live in fear when factory workers like Sophie's papá fed America.

Sophie wanted to help her family and other families like hers. When she was given the chance to go to Washington, DC, to see the pope, she was determined to use the opportunity to make a difference. During his trip, Pope Francis was driven through the heart of the city so he could wave to the people. With a letter clutched in her fist, Sophie darted through the crowd and slipped past the parade barrier, racing out into the road. Suddenly a man dressed in a black suit appeared. The pope had beckoned for Sophie to come meet him! With a kind smile, Pope Francis hugged Sophie and accepted her heartfelt letter.

The pope took her letter to the US Congress. He asked that undocumented parents of American citizens, like Sophie, be protected. Sophie became an icon of immigration reform, but she was just getting started. At five years old, she knew she had a lifetime of activism ahead of her.

BORN DECEMBER 17, 2010
UNITED STATES OF AMERICA

"I HAVE A RIGHT TO BE HAPPY."
—SOPHIE CRUZ

ILLUSTRATION BY
GABY VERDOOREN

TAEGEN YARDLEY

ANIMAL RIGHTS ACTIVIST AND FILMMAKER

Once upon a time, a 12-year-old girl was shocked to learn that elephants were endangered. Sitting in her classroom, Taegen imagined a future without elephants—those gentle giants with sparkling intelligence and deeply sensitive souls. Her heart broke. But instead of sinking under her sadness, Taegen took action.

First, she educated herself. Elephants were killed so their ivory tusks could be carved into jewelry. Though many countries had banned the sale of ivory, it continued, often illegally, all over the world.

Next, she made a film to share everything she had learned. In it, Taegen recounted the story of Lawrence Anthony, an elephant rescuer in South Africa, who passed away in 2012. After his passing, a group of wild elephants Lawrence had saved traveled miles through the scorching hot desert to his house. They remained for two days, paying solemn respect to their beloved savior.

Since that first film, Taegen has made five more about endangered species and habitats. Through organizing marches and bake sales, she's inspired her community to stand up for animals. She's spoken before the United Nations and the National Geographic Society. Taegan even got to meet Prince William, the Duke of Cambridge, when she received an award for her conservation work.

No matter what adventures lie ahead, she'll never forget what the elephants first taught her: *lead with your heart.*

BORN FEBRUARY 6, 2003
UNITED STATES OF AMERICA

"MAY WE NEVER STOP ASKING OURSELVES, 'IF NOT ME, THEN WHO?'"
—TAEGEN YARDLEY

ILLUSTRATION BY JIALEI SUN

TANYARADZWA "TANYA" MUZINDA

MOTOCROSS RACER

Vroom! A girl raced up on a motorbike. She was five years old, she lived in Zimbabwe, and she had found the sport for her. Her name was Tanyaradzwa, and everyone called her Tanya.

Tanya's dad was a former biker. He got her started with a go-kart, but it wasn't long before she traded in four wheels for two. Tanya's dad gave her her first motorbike, breaking the tradition of gifting a bike to the firstborn boy in the family. Some family members didn't understand why a girl should have a motorbike. Tanya didn't care. *Vroom!* Off she went, her lime-green helmet speeding away and bobbing over the rolling dirt hills at the local motosport park.

Eventually, Tanya zoomed all the way to local and then international tournaments. Most of the time, she was the only girl there. At the starting line, she would look out over the millions of tire marks in the soft dirt, take a deep breath, and press the gas. She'd race to the finish line, whooshing by all the others. At six years old, Tanya became the first Zimbabwean female motocross champion in history.

Tanya loves to race, but she also loves the opportunities motocross gives her. When her helmet's off, Tanya helps other children—especially girls—go to school by giving donations and sharing her prize money. "Most of the children I paid for are girls because when parents don't have enough money to send their kids to school, they'd prefer to send the boy child," she said. As Tanya races toward her goals, she's bringing other girls along for the ride.

BORN AUGUST 31, 2004

ZIMBABWE

"OTHER WOMEN HAD TO FIGHT AND ACHIEVE THE RIGHT FOR US TO BE WHERE WE ARE RIGHT NOW."
—TANYARADZWA "TANYA" MUZINDA

ILLUSTRATION BY DOMINIQUE RAMSEY

TAYLOR SWIFT

SINGER-SONGWRITER

Once there was a girl with scars on the tips of her fingers. From the time she was 12 years old, Taylor would play the guitar for hours. She knew what it felt like to be an outcast and to have her heart broken. So she wove her emotions and experiences into her songs and then dreamed up melodies to match. And when her fingers bled, she would tape them up and keep plucking away at the strings.

Taylor convinced her family to move from Pennsylvania to Nashville, Tennessee, so she could become a country star. There she played at every café or barbecue that would allow her. She asked everyone to call radio stations and request her songs. Soon people began to notice the incredible lyrics and harmonies of the young girl with golden curls.

At 16, Taylor got a record deal and released her first album. It was a hit, and she became the youngest person to write and sing a number one song all on her own! After winning many, many awards, Taylor showcased her talents by producing record-breaking pop, rock, and folk albums. Any time people doubted her, she proved them wrong by surprising them with a new sound or a clever line.

As one of the most powerful artists in the business, Taylor stands up for women, especially in the music industry, and the LGBTQIA+ community. In 2018, her plea to Tennessee voters to fight for equality inspired 65,000 people to register to vote.

"No matter what happens in life, be good to people," she says. "Being good to people is a wonderful legacy to leave behind."

BORN DECEMBER 13, 1989
UNITED STATES OF AMERICA

ILLUSTRATION BY
ANNA DIXON

"I WANT TO STILL
HAVE A SHARP PEN
AND A THIN SKIN
AND AN OPEN HEART."
—TAYLOR SWIFT

TE MANAIA JENNINGS

PAINTER AND MENTAL HEALTH ADVOCATE

There once was a girl who discovered how to channel her big feelings into art. When Te Manaia was little, she spent a lot of time in the hospital. She was diagnosed with a rare condition called congenital scoliosis, which causes her spine to curve sideways. While the physical pain she felt from her surgeries was intense, her anxiety and depression hurt the most.

Lying in bed in the hospital, Te Manaia decided that she needed an outlet to cope with the challenges she was facing. Drawing and painting calmed her. She painted faces in moody shades of purple and blue. Sometimes the people in her paintings were crying, sometimes they were smiling, and sometimes they were serious. Slowly, Te Manaia started to feel differently about her body and about herself. Painting also became a way for her to explore her Indigenous heritage. She began incorporating Māori designs into her art.

Te Manaia's interest in art and mental health became intertwined. "I saw an opportunity to be a voice for young people, especially young Māori people, and to normalize conversations around mental health and just say: 'It's OK to be sad. It's OK to not always feel good.' Everyone has bad days," Te Manaia says.

Art not only helped Te Manaia cope with her negative feelings, but it also changed the way she thinks about her body. "I like my scars now, and I like showing them off because it shows strength," she says. "It shows my story."

BORN JANUARY 3, 2000
NEW ZEALAND

"I WANT PEOPLE TO SEE THE STRENGTH WITHIN THEMSELVES."
—TE MANAIA JENNINGS

ILLUSTRATION BY
STORY HEMI-MOREHOUSE

TEMILAYO ABODUNRIN

SAXOPHONIST

Once upon a time at a concert, a Nigerian keyboardist named Temilayo became enchanted by the smooth sounds of a saxophone. Even though she'd traveled from church to church playing the keyboard, there was something magical about the saxophone.

At six years old, she decided to learn that instrument too.

For Temilayo, weekdays were for schoolwork, but weekends were for music. Nothing could separate her from her sax! Temilayo learned quickly, and soon she was playing her new instrument at weddings while brides and grooms danced under twinkling lights. She played at churches where people clapped to her music between sermons. Because of her age, the audience expected her to play nursery rhymes like "Mary Had a Little Lamb." Instead, she wowed them with complex, jazzy tunes. Other people's expectations never made Temilayo doubt herself. She even started posting videos of herself online playing her own versions of popular tunes.

Churches and weddings turned into big stages. Temilayo shared the spotlight with famous Nigerian artists like Johnny Drille, Wole Oni, and Davido. In 2020, she recorded "Ayo," a song she'd written, with other award-winning musicians. The video for "Ayo" shows the young musician in colorful clothes, grooving to the beat.

Temilayo followed the sound of the saxophone, and her curiosity led her to countless new opportunities, all because she was brave enough to try something new.

BORN NOVEMBER 19, 2009

NIGERIA

"I WANT MY MUSIC TO
MAKE MY AUDIENCE
HAPPY, SMILE, INSPIRED,
BELIEVE IN THEMSELVES."
—TEMILAYO ABODUNRIN

ILLUSTRATION BY
RAFAELA RIJO-NÚÑEZ

THEODORA VON LIECHTENSTEIN

CONSERVATIONIST

Once upon a time, in the rolling green hills of Liechtenstein, there lived a real-life princess named Theodora. She grew up with her royal family in a castle that looked like it came right out of a fairy tale. Like make-believe princesses Snow White and Aurora, Theodora loved animals. "Animals help me to relax," she said. "They help me stay calm."

But Theodora was crestfallen when she realized how much of the wildlife on Earth was endangered. With the destruction of habitats and rising pollution, so many creatures were struggling. After doing some research, Princess Theodora found that a lot of these problems could be solved if people made small changes in how they treat nature.

She created her own foundation to educate teens about the importance of environmental conservation. She founded the Green Teen Team when she was nine years old and began working with teens all around the world to help safeguard wildlife. One of the projects she worked on was the Chelonia Project, which provided a healthy habitat for endangered tortoises in Italy. Theodora and her team built a protected habitat for European pond turtles. Seeing them basking on the banks, their smooth black shells with tiny yellow spots shining in the sun, makes her happy.

Theodora believes that if young people can learn about the impact they can have on the environment and the animals in it, they can work toward giving all living things a better future.

BORN NOVEMBER 20, 2004

LIECHTENSTEIN AND ITALY

"IF PEOPLE DON'T TAKE YOUNG ACTIVISTS SERIOUSLY, THEN MAYBE THEY ARE NOT REALLY LISTENING TO WHAT WE ARE SAYING."
—THEODORA VON LIECHTENSTEIN

ILLUSTRATION BY SOFIA CAVALLARI

TRANG

COMEDIAN AND YOUTUBER

Trang lived with her family in a small thatched hut in rural Vietnam. She helped her mother sell sweet cakes at the market across the river. One day, their boat tipped over, and all their cakes tumbled into the water. Trang's mother cried, knowing they wouldn't have enough money to buy food.

"I will never forget that day," Trang recalled. "I wanted so badly to help my family out of poverty." She sat and thought. She had a special bond with animals, especially with Bim Bim. He was the only white duck in a flock of all black birds, and he was not accepted by the group. *Bim Bim must be lonely*, thought Trang, *just like me*. It dawned on her that maybe, just maybe, the world might enjoy their unique friendship.

Trang had heard about YouTube. She dreamed of becoming an actor and decided to start her own channel. "At first, I recorded videos with old phones that kept on breaking," she said. "Many times my videos didn't get a single view." But Trang kept at it. She posted Bim Bim's birthday party, Bim Bim learning to cook, and Bim Bim dancing. Over time, the whole nation was laughing along.

Trang won YouTube's Silver Button Award for earning 100,000 fans. "I never thought I could go that far. I do not have an assistant. I do not have high quality equipment," she said. "I taught myself everything."

Trang hopes her success inspires others to think beyond what feels possible.

BORN 2002
VIETNAM

00:15:28

"IF YOU FALL, YOU WILL GROW UP."
—TRANG

ILLUSTRATION BY
JUNETIEN

VANESSA NAKATE

CLIMATE ACTIVIST

Vanessa grew up near the Congo Basin, the second largest rain forest on Earth. The area was home to thousands of plants and animals, like the Colobus monkey, which has long fur that looks like wings when it jumps from tree to tree, and the okapi, a forest giraffe with striped legs that can't be found anywhere else on Earth.

Vanessa loved where she lived.

She watched her father plant trees all over Uganda as the leader of an environmental organization. His work encouraged Vanessa to get involved. When the Congo rain forest caught fire, she began to speak out. Vanessa took her message to shopping malls. She talked about saving the rain forest in front of fossil fuel stations and in front of Parliament. Sometimes, she was the only one to show up to a protest.

People said she was wasting her time.

But she kept going, because she believed in what she was fighting for. Vanessa's words started to inspire people. In one article, she wrote, "Our environment is our inheritance. And we have to protect it, or we face the consequences." She was invited to speak around the world, including at the 2019 UN Climate Change Conference.

Vanessa knows she's not alone in fighting for environmental justice in Africa. She founded the Rise Up Climate Movement and Youth for Future Africa to uplift and support activists around the continent fighting for a greener tomorrow.

BORN NOVEMBER 15, 1996

UGANDA

"YOUR ACTIONS MATTER.
NO ACTION OR VOICE IS
TOO SMALL TO MAKE
A DIFFERENCE."
—VANESSA NAKATE

ILLUSTRATION BY
NAKI NARH

VICTORIA ALONSOPEREZ

ENGINEER AND INVENTOR

Victoria was always fascinated by math. Her dad was an accountant, and she would peer over his shoulder as he worked, trying to make sense of all the formulas. Her dad told her that numbers could be used in all sorts of ways, including getting astronauts to the moon! Victoria knew then that she wanted to use numbers to build something amazing.

When she was 12 years old, Victoria saw her chance. A frightening disease was spreading across farms in Uruguay, where she lived. Cows, sheep, and goats were getting sick and there wasn't enough meat or milk to go around. No one knew what to do. But Victoria started brainstorming.

Cows don't act normally when they're sick, she thought to herself. *They can't eat, they drool, and they feel warm. They can't make milk.* That's when a light bulb seemed to light up over her head. *POP! What if there is a way to keep track of how cows are feeling?* Victoria pondered. *That way, we could stop the illness from spreading.*

Years later, after graduating as an electrical engineer, Victoria began to sketch out the design for a product she called the Chipsafer, a system that could track the physical changes in livestock through a special GPS-enabled collar and alert farmers through an app on their phone or computer. Victoria entered her idea into a competition for young inventors like herself. She won, and now, she works with farmers in Latin America, building the business she dreamed of as a little girl.

BORN OCTOBER 22, 1987
URUGUAY

ILLUSTRATION BY
NATALIA CARDONA PUERTA

"I WOULD LIKE TO SEE
MORE INNOVATION
OCCURRING IN LATIN
AMERICA."
—VICTORIA ALONSOPEREZ

VINISHA UMASHANKAR

ENVIRONMENTAL ACTIVIST AND INVENTOR

Once there was a girl whose daily walk home from school gave her a big idea. Vinisha often watched people walk through the sunny streets of her hometown, Tiruvannamalai, India. It made her happy to see them stop and talk to friends and vendors.

But one day, Vinisha noticed an ironing cart owner throwing away loads of charcoal. Around 10 million ironers set up their carts along busy roads across India every morning. They use portable irons to make people's clothes look crisp. The only problem is, these irons are not electric. They don't plug in to an energy source. They're little metal boxes that vendors fill with burning charcoal to heat up and press clothes flat.

Vinisha was surprised to learn that smoke from the charcoal-burning carts contributed to climate change and lung problems like cancer, so she began to think of ways to avoid creating all that pollution. The hot sun was part of the problem, making it impossible to keep clothes clean and wrinkle-free, but Vinisha saw a way it could help too . . . solar power!

She designed a new kind of cart—one with a solar panel roof. The panels would keep the irons hot, and the roof would keep the ironers in the shade. The cart Vinisha designed was so revolutionary that she won the Children's Climate Prize. She plans to start manufacturing it soon.

Vinisha is hopeful that clearing the air in her city will make life better for her friends and family, as well as generations to come.

BORN OCTOBER 11, 2006

INDIA

"WHEN IT COMES TO CLIMATE CHANGE, THERE IS NO STOP BUTTON."
—VINISHA UMASHANKAR

ILLUSTRATION BY
TASNEEM AMIRUDDIN

VITÓRIA BUENO

BALLERINA

O nce there was a girl who always had a bounce in her step. Before she even knew it, she was dancing.

Vitória was born without arms, but as she says, "for me, arms, they're just a detail. I don't feel like I need them at all." Other people may rely on their arms to do the dishes or brush their teeth, and yet Vitória can do all these things and more—using her feet!

Things weren't always easy for Vitória. When she was really tiny, she didn't have the strength or flexibility to grab the hood of her sweatshirt with her toe and yank it up over her head. And when she walked along the streets of rural Brazil where she grew up, nosy neighbors would approach her to tug on the sleeves of her shirt.

One day, when Vitória was five years old, her physiotherapist noticed that bounce in her step. It was clear that she liked to dance.

Maybe you would like to give ballet a try? the therapist asked.

Vitória and ballet clicked immediately. She moved her body to the music with elegance and grace. When other girls raised their arms up in the air, she straightened her neck long and tilted her head up—she found she didn't really need arms to echo their movements. She was a natural! By the time she was 16, she was jumping and twirling on stages all over the world.

"I think I was born to dance," Vitória says. "I was born to dance ballet."

BORN MARCH 2004

BRAZIL

"WE ARE MORE THAN OUR
DISABILITIES, SO WE HAVE
TO CHASE OUR DREAMS."
—VITÓRIA BUENO

XÓCHITL GUADALUPE CRUZ LÓPEZ

INVENTOR

In Los Altos de Chiapas in the mountains of Mexico, where it is cold for most of the year, there lived a little girl named Xóchitl. People were constantly getting sick and having to go to the doctor. Xóchitl was only seven years old, but she worried about her older neighbors.

She also noticed that, in order to take warm baths, many of the people in her town chopped down beautiful trees to use for firewood because there were no affordable heaters for them to buy. The fires heated their water but destroyed their forests. *How can I make a heater without harming the environment?* she thought to herself. The answer that came to her was simple: use people's trash!

Xóchitl took out her sketchbook and spent weeks working on a design for a water heater. She painted 10 water bottles black to trap heat from the sun. Then she connected them with 50 feet of black hose. She attached the bottles to a complicated structure made of discarded plastic, wood, nylon, and glass cooler doors. Her dad helped her install the project on the roof of their house. When it was all done, Xóchitl added up what she'd spent. Her heater had cost just $30 to build. Even better, it did exactly what it was supposed to do.

People all over Mexico read about her project, amazed that a young girl had come up with such a practical and helpful invention. She even won an award that was given every year to outstanding women scientists. It had never been given to a kid before!

BORN JANUARY 1, 2009

MEXICO

"PEOPLE WON'T HAVE TO CHOP DOWN TREES TO HEAT THEIR WATER ANYMORE."
—XÓCHITL GUADALUPE CRUZ LÓPEZ

ILLUSTRATION BY REN CAPACIO

YASHIKA

KARATE CHAMPION

Once upon a time, there was a girl who karate-chopped her fear. For young Yashika, getting to school was scary. Without streetlights, sidewalks, or school buses, the route was sometimes dangerous. Yashika's parents worried so much that they asked her to stop going. But She was determined to get an education. Yashika knew there had to be a safe way to get to school. Instead of giving up, she asked local leaders for help, and they listened.

Yashika was given the opportunity to take a self-defense class for girls. Standing in front of the class was the teacher, a powerful and strong woman. *If she can do it, why not me?* Yashika thought to herself.

People in her town teased Yashika and her family. *Karate is a boy's sport,* they'd say. Her parents pressed her to quit, but Yashika continued to train. "By doing karate, I learned to never give up, no matter my challenges," she said. Before she knew it, Yashika won a tournament! Then another and another.

A few years later, Yashika boarded a train and traveled to the biggest city in all of India to compete in a national karate championship. There, the girl who was once afraid of walking to school won a silver medal for her individual performance and, with her team, she won a gold.

Today, the Karate Girl, as she is called by her fans, is a beloved mentor for girls. She tells her students that dedication, focus, and hard work will make dreams come true, and karate will help them kick fear's butt!

BORN 2003

INDIA

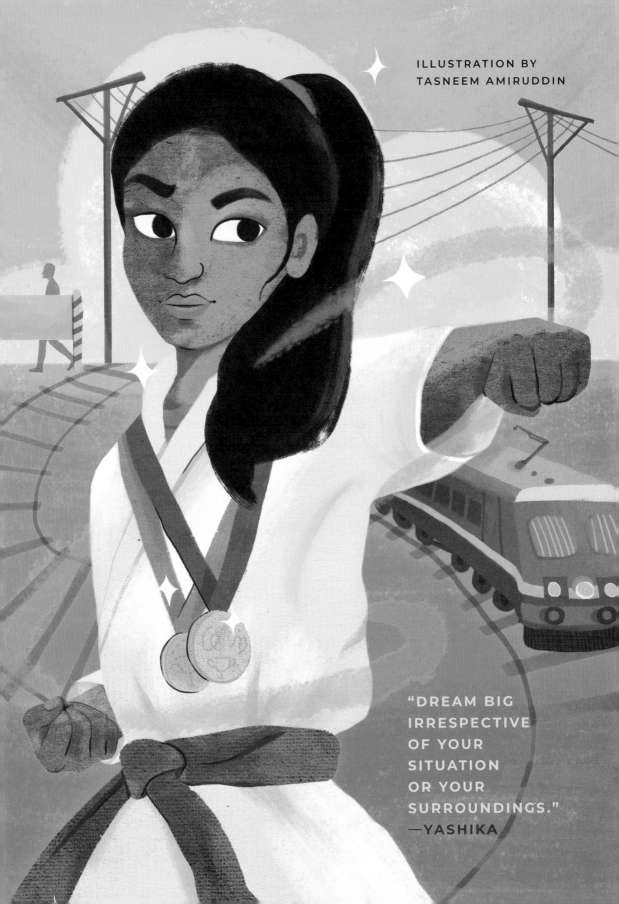

ILLUSTRATION BY
TASNEEM AMIRUDDIN

"DREAM BIG
IRRESPECTIVE
OF YOUR
SITUATION
OR YOUR
SURROUNDINGS."
—YASHIKA

ZENDAYA

ACTOR AND SINGER

Once upon a time in the bustling, seaside city of Oakland, California, there was a shy girl who found her voice through the magic of theater.

Zendaya was so shy in fact that she had to repeat kindergarten because she just couldn't speak up during class. But when she started to accompany her mom to her job at a local theater, things changed.

Every night, Zendaya would eat dinner backstage with the actors, then set up a cozy spot with pillows and blankets in the back of the theater and watch the show. She loved it all: the lights, the costumes, the music. Soon Zendaya was taking theater classes and performing too.

As she grew up, Zendaya jumped from the stage to the screen, taking on more exciting roles. She played a trapeze artist flying through the air and was even cast as Spiderman's iconic best friend. In 2020, Zendaya became the youngest actor ever to win an Emmy award for outstanding female lead in a drama series.

Zendaya has become more confident with each role and Hollywood event. The girl who was too shy to say a word in kindergarten now lets her personality shine. She once went to a gala wearing a light blue, light-up Cinderella ball gown and carrying a glittery pumpkin carriage purse. And she isn't afraid to speak her mind. She uses her voice to address important issues, like racial discrimination: "I want to be a part of the change," she says. "It's important that creatives of all races, if they have an opportunity or platform, use it to make room for other people."

BORN SEPTEMBER 1, 1996
UNITED STATES OF AMERICA

ILLUSTRATION BY
TYLER MISHÁ
BARNETT

"DON'T TRY SO HARD TO
FIT IN, AND CERTAINLY
DON'T TRY SO HARD TO BE
DIFFERENT . . . JUST TRY
HARD TO BE YOU."
—ZENDAYA

MEET MORE REBELS!

In the Good Night Stories for Rebel Girls series, we celebrate the accomplishments of many young Rebels. Here are some of the other girls and young women whose stories uplift, energize, and inspire.

AISHOLPAN NURGAIV

Once there was a 13-year-old girl named Aisholpan who raised an eaglet. She was the first woman to enter the Golden Eagle competition in Mongolia.

Illustration by Sally Nixon

AMANDA GORMAN

As a little girl with a speech impediment, Amanda discovered the power of poetry. Later, she read a poem to the world as the youngest poet at a US presidential inauguration.

Illustration by Keturah Ariel

ANN MAKOSINSKI

Ann once visited a home without electricity. She was shocked. At 15 years old, she invented a flashlight that runs on body heat.

Illustration by Claudia Carieri

BALKISSA CHAIBOU

When Balkissa was 12 years old, she was told she had to get married. She fought her family in court. The judge ruled in her favor, and she went to university to study medicine.

Illustration by Priya Kuriyan

BANA ALABED

Bana was seven years old when her city, Aleppo, was attacked. She bravely reported her experiences online so the public could see what was happening in Syria.

Illustration by Tatheer Syeda

BEATRICE VIO

After a bout with meningitis, Bebe had to have her legs and forearms amputated. A talented athlete, she is the only wheelchair fencer in the world without limbs.

Illustration by Cristina Portolano

COY MATHIS

Coy knew she was a girl even though she was assigned male at birth. Her school district discriminated against her. And a judge decided she could use the girls bathroom at school.

Illustration by Marta Lorenzon

GABBY DOUGLAS

When she was little, Gabby could do handstands, splits, and one-handed cartwheels! She was the first Black gymnast to become an individual all-around Olympic champion.

Illustration by Adriana Bellet

JAWAHIR JEWELS ROBLE

Once there was a girl named JJ who would play soccer in the street using a potato for a ball. She grew up to be the first female Muslim soccer referee in the UK.

Illustration by Veronica Ruffato

JESSICA WATSON

Once there was a girl named Jessica who sailed around the world. At age 16, she completed the journey all on her own.

Illustration by Kathrin Honesta

KHERIS ROGERS

When Kheris was teased for her dark skin, she decided to "flex in her complexion." She launched an online movement and a series of T-shirts to uplift other girls like her.

Illustration by Maya Ealey

KHOUDIA DIOP

Khoudia didn't let childhood insults about her complexion prevent her from becoming a model. She called herself the Melanin Goddess!

Illustration by Debora Guidi

MARSAI MARTIN

Once there was a girl named Marsai who pitched her movie idea to the right people. At 13, she became the youngest executive producer in Hollywood.

Illustration by Keisha Okafor

MC SOFFIA

Soffia wanted Black girls to love and accept themselves. She wrote a song called "Menina Pretinha," or "Little Black Girl," which made her an internet sensation.

Illustration by Keisha Okafor

MICHAELA DEPRINCE

Michaela was teased for having a skin condition called vitiligo, but she focused on her dream of dancing. At 18, she joined the Dutch National Ballet.

Illustration by Debora Guidi

MUZOON ALMELLEHAN

Muzoon would not let the Syrian war stop her from getting an education. She settled in England and joined UNICEF as a goodwill ambassador.

Illustration by Maliha Abidi

NADIA MURAD

Once upon a time, 20-year-old Nadia escaped from terrorist captors in Iraq. She spoke up and told her story to the United Nations.

Illustration by Ping Zhu

NANDI BUSHELL

Once upon a time, there was a girl named Nandi, who never missed a beat. At age 11, she played drums and got into a rock battle with legendary drummer Dave Grohl.

Illustration by Sharee Miller

NAOMI OSAKA

Naomi has trained to be a tennis player since she was three years old. At 20, she won the 2018 US Open against her idol, Serena Williams.

Illustration by Danielle Elysse Mann

POORNA MALAVATH

Poorna wanted to climb the highest mountain in the world. At 13, she became the youngest girl to make it to the top of Mount Everest.

Illustration by Priya Kuriyan

PHIONA MUTESI

Phiona won her first chess championship when she was 11. There is even a movie about her! Now, she teaches other kids how to play chess too.

Illustration by Onyinye Iwu

SAMARRIA BREVARD

Once there was a girl named Samarria who spent all her time at the skate parks. She mastered a trick called the tre flip and won a silver medal at the X Games.

Illustration by Sharee Miller

SIMONE BILES

Once upon a time, a girl named Simone learned to twist and turn in the air. The world's most decorated gymnast, she's also an advocate for mental health in sports.

Illustration by Eline van Dam

SIMONE MANUEL

Simone competed in the 100-meter race at 19 years old. She became the first Black woman to win an Olympic gold medal in swimming.

Illustration by Danielle Elysse Mann

SKY BROWN

Once there was a 13-year-old girl named Sky who performed amazing stunts on her skateboard. Her skills made her Great Britain's youngest Olympic medalist.

Illustration by Kate Prior

SONITA ALIZADEH

Sonita wrote a rap song protesting against arranged marriage. The video went viral, and her message was heard around the world.

Illustration by Samidha Gunjal

THOKOZILE MUWAMBA

Thokozile wanted to see the world from the sky. She spent years in flight training and became the first female fighter pilot in Zambia.

Illustration by Ashleigh Corrin

XIYE BASTIDA

When 17-year-old Xiye realized how climate change hurt Indigenous people, she started a strike at her school. Under her leadership, 600 students walked out.

Illustration by Sally Deng

YEONMI PARK

Yeonmi was not free to express herself under North Korea's repressive regime. After escaping at 14, she fought to liberate her birth country with a speech at the One Young World Summit.

Illustration by Joana Estrela

YUSRA MARDINI

When a boat full of Syrian refugees broke down, Yusra jumped into the water and guided it to safety. She soon joined a swim team—the first refugee team to compete in the Olympics.

Illustration by Jessica Cooper

Rebel Girls also publishes themed collections of inspiring stories. Here are some of the amazing girls and young women from our mini books.

ALY RAISMAN

Aly captained a team of gymnasts at the Olympics in 2012 and 2016. Both times, she led her squad to win an all-around gold medal.

Illustration by Salini Perera

ARIARNE TITMUS

By age 12, Ariarne was winning swim meets. At the Olympic Games in Tokyo, she won gold and broke a world record in freestyle.

Illustration by Sol Cotti

AUTUMN PELTIER

Autumn learned of contaminated water at the reserve where she lived. She voiced her concern to Canada's prime minister at a gathering for First Nations communities.

Illustration by Jing Li

BRIGETTE LACQUETTE

Once there was a girl named Brigette who loved being on the ice. She joined the Canadian women's hockey team as the first First Nations player.

Illustration by Maya McKibbin

CHARLOTTE WORTHINGTON

Charlotte dreamed of nailing a 360 backflip on her bike. She did—making her the first Olympic gold medalist in women's freestyle BMX.

Illustration by Lydia MBA

CHLOE KIM

Once upon a time, a girl named Chloe did flips on her snowboard. At 14, she became the youngest athlete to win a medal at the winter X Games.

Illustration by Salini Perera

ELLA AND CAITLIN MCEWAN

Once there were sisters named Ella and Caitlin who started a petition to ban plastic toys in kids' meals. They collected half a million signatures!

Illustration by Anine Bösenberg

ESOHE OZIGBO

Esohe wanted to bring attention to the trash that littered Nigeria. She created a "trashion show," making outfits out of plastic bags and other discarded materials.

Illustration by Ronique Ellis

FLEUR JONG

Fleur sprints and leaps on special blades. She broke the long jump world record at the World Para Athletics Championships.

Illustration by Mia Saine

JAMIE MARGOLIN

Once upon a time, a girl named Jamie fought for a healthier planet. At 17, she formed a movement with young activists around the world called Zero Hour.

Illustration by Pau Zamro

LINA AND SANNA EL KOTT HELANDER

Identical twins Lina and Sanna discovered a new sport: skyrunning. Now, they race up mountains and win awards all around the globe.

Illustration by Jennifer Berglund

MALALA YOUSAFZAI

Malala fought for girls' education—and her life. At 17, she became the youngest person ever to receive the Nobel Peace Prize.

Illustration by Sara Bondi

MIHO NONAKA

Once there was a girl named Miho who scrambled up giant rocks. At 21, she won the overall bouldering title at the Climbing World Cup.

Illustration by Salini Perera

MYA-ROSE CRAIG

Once there was a girl named Mya-Rose who watched every bird she could. She saw half of the world's birds by the time she was 11!

Illustration by Julia Kuo

PAIGE BROWN

Paige saw that toxic algal blooms were killing frogs in streams. So she invented a water filter. Later, she founded a company that makes weather-forecasting balloons.

Illustration by Alexandra Filipek

SARAH FULLER

Sarah loved soccer—and football too! She earned a spot as the first woman to play in the Power Five, the highest level of college football.

Illustration by Carmen Casado

SUNI LEE

The first Hmong American athlete to compete in the Olympics, Suni was also the first Asian American gymnast to win gold in the all-around event.

Illustration by Danielle Elysse Mann

TEGAN VINCENT-COOKE

Once there was a girl with cerebral palsy who mastered the art of dressage. She aims to be the first Black woman to represent Great Britain in Paralympic equestrianism.

Illustration by DeAndra Hodge

GLOSSARY

BIOMEDICAL ENGINEERING (noun) — a field that concentrates on designing technology to help people who are hurt or sick

COLORISM (noun) — discrimination of a group of people, often within an ethnic group, based on skin color or features such as eye and hair color

CYBERSECURITY (noun) — actions taken or applications created to protect a computer or device from online attacks

DEFORESTATION (noun) — the act of removing a large area of trees

DYSLEXIA (noun) — a learning issue where a person has trouble connecting letters, making it tough to read, write, or spell

GYNECOLOGIST (noun) — a doctor who specializes in the health of women and their reproductive organs

HACKATHON (noun) — an event where people come together to build, design, and code new computer programs

HIJAB (noun) — a traditional head and neck covering worn by Muslim women

IMMIGRANT (noun) — a person who comes to a country to live there permanently

INCLUSIVE (adjective) — to include and accommodate people of all races, genders, sexualities, and abilities

INDIGENOUS (adjective) — relating to people who are the original inhabitants of an area or their descendants

MECHANICAL ENGINEERING (noun) — a field that focuses on how things are made, especially regarding aspects of force or motion

NEUROVASCULAR (adjective) — relating to blood vessels and nerves

PHYSIOTHERAPIST (noun) — a professional who helps people with movement, often treating injuries

PROTOTYPE (noun) — a basic model used to test out an idea or concept

REFUGEE (noun) — a person who is forced to leave their country because of war, exile, or natural disaster or for political or religious reasons

SOCIAL ENTREPRENEUR (noun) — someone who starts a business in order to solve societal, cultural, environmental, or community-based problems

SOCIAL JUSTICE (noun) — the view that everyone deserves equal access to wealth, privileges, and opportunities

TRANSGENDER (adjective) — when a person's gender identity is not the same as the one assigned at birth

UNDOCUMENTED (adjective) — lacking the appropriate immigration or working papers

WRITE YOUR OWN STORY

Once upon a time, _____

_____

_____

_____

_____

_____

_____

_____

_____

_____

_____

_____

_____

_____

_____

_____

_____

_____

_____

_____

_____

_____

_____

_____

DRAW YOUR OWN PORTRAIT

BE THE HOST

Talk show host Keke Palmer knows that interviewing people is an art. Have you ever daydreamed about having your own talk show or asking your idols questions on the red carpet or your own podcast? Here's your chance!

1. Make a list of people, living or dead, who you would love to meet and learn more about. (Maybe some of them are in this book!)

2. Choose three and prep your interview with them.

3. Do some research on each of them so you can reference their talents and accomplishments in your chat.

4. Write up the questions you would like to ask.

5. Pick one interview and use your imagination to write an entire scene—with both your questions and your guest's answers.

6. Turn your scene into a play, like the one Isabella Madrigal wrote. Ask a friend or family member to act it out with you.

INVENT FOR EVERYONE!

Isabella Springmühl creates clothing that looks great and is comfortable for customers with Down syndrome. Riya Karamanchi designed a smart cane for the visually impaired. They are champions of inclusive design.

1. Make a list of the things you do every day or every week.

2. Think about people with abilities that are different from yours. Would it be easy for someone with a visual or hearing impairment to get around your school or participate in the same hobbies as you? Would a person who uses a wheelchair or has a chronic illness find it easy to participate in the after-school activities you enjoy?

3. Design a solution that would make it easier or more fun for more people to do the activities you are used to doing.

UPDATE A CLASSIC

One day, Maayan Segal asked her father why the king was worth more than the queen in a deck of playing cards. After that, she set out on a quest to redesign a simple set of cards to make them more inclusive and reflect a more equal society. Can you think of another game that needs an update? How would you change it and why?

RECORD THE WORLD

Bonnie Chiu and Liina Heikkinen know all about the power of photography—to capture the joy and humanity in people's everyday lives and to share the wonders of nature. What images move you the most? What will you explore with your camera?

1. Brainstorm a list of people and/or places you would like to photograph.

2. Make a plan with your grown-ups to go on a picture-taking adventure. Maybe they would like to snap memorable photos too?

3. Go out into the world to record your memories in pictures.

COMMIT TO HELPFUL HABITS

Think of ways your photography could help others. Perhaps you would like to share smiles and stories with older adults, like Ruby Kate Chitsey? You might offer to take portraits at an assisted living home. Are you an animal lover, like Shaine Kilyun? Maybe you could help a nearby animal rescue by snapping sweet shots of pets up for adoption. Or maybe you want to record the wonders of nature by taking pictures of worms emerging on a rainy day or the flowers blooming at the local park. The possibilities are endless!

FACE YOUR FEARS

Rebecca Roos Jensen was terrified of riding in planes. To get over her fear of flying, she studied to become a pilot. Mikaila Ulmer was afraid of bees before she started her own honey-sweetened lemonade company. Think about something you are afraid of. Brainstorm ways to get over your fear. Then write a story about confronting your fear. Picture each moment in your head, and don't forget to include the details.

ABOUT THE AUTHORS

AMA KWARTENG (author) is a fiction writer, the beauty editor at the digital publication *Coveteur*, and a contributing fiction editor for *Story* magazine. She graduated from Barnard College in 2017 with a degree in anthropology. Her academic background allows her to view the beauty world through a unique perspective.

AVERY GIRION (author) is an award-winning writer and experienced writers' assistant with a love for comedy, television, and telling female-focused stories. She studied at Chapman University where she cofounded the school's first satire paper, and now resides in Los Angeles, where she writes and performs comedy.

BINDI IRWIN (foreword) is a passionate wildlife conservationist, who has inherited her parents' love for wildlife and wild places. Born to Wildlife Warriors Steve and Terri Irwin, Bindi is a determined soul, destined to make a positive difference on the planet. Australia Zoo has always been her home. Every animal is part of her family. As Bindi has grown, so has her passion for conservation. She has traveled the world, visiting wild places, to learn more about the planet she wants to protect into the future. Through Wildlife Warriors, Bindi continues to work with her family to share the message of conservation.

EMILY CONNER (author) is a 16-year-old writer and graphic designer in Florida. She writes poems, stories, and journalistic essays. She has been a Girl Scout since she was five years old. An activist and community volunteer, she founded the literary art magazine *Astraea Zine*.

FRANCES THOMAS (author) is a writer and editor based in Brooklyn, New York. She loves going to the movies on weekday afternoons, cooking big dinners with friends, and reading stories aloud to her husband. In everything she writes, she hopes to empower readers to become their biggest, truest selves.

JESS HARRITON (editor and author) is an editor at Rebel Girls, working on stories to delight and inspire girls 7 to 12. Previously, she was an editor at Penguin Random House, where she worked with best-selling and award-winning authors. Her writing has appeared in *Concrete Literary Magazine* and HelloGiggles.com. Jess graduated from Emerson College in 2013. She lives in Brooklyn, New York, in an apartment filled with books.

MAITHY VU (editor and author) is a Vietnamese American writer who loves surrealism and most things odd. While earning her BA in theater arts at the University of California, Santa Cruz, she spent time writing poetry, plays, and slightly bizarre sketches for an all-women comedy team. Maithy published her novella, *Wounded Wisteria*, in 2015, combining fiction in verse with her own watercolor illustrations. She earned her MLA in creative writing and literature at Harvard Extension School, where she completed her first novel, *Squid Season*. In early 2019, Maithy joined the editorial team at Rebel Girls. Since then, her colleagues have been given compulsory lectures about Taylor Swift on a weekly basis.

SAM GUSS (author) is a children's book author, playwright, researcher, and narrative shaper who works with visual artists and technologists on interactive art installations. She is the cocreator of *Feminist Flashcards*, published by Downtown Bookworks. Some of her other stories can be found in *Rebel Girls Champions*, *Rebel Girls Powerful Pairs*, and *Rebel Girls Climate Warriors*. She lives in Brooklyn, New York.

SHANNON JADE (author) is a writer who believes in the real-world magic of storytelling. She is the author of *Seashells for Stories*, *Way Back When*, and several other fiction books and projects. Shannon holds a BA in creative writing, professional writing, and publishing from Curtin University and is currently studying for a master's degree in environment. Shannon hopes the magical worlds that appear in her stories will one day help us all save our own magical world.

SHELBI POLK (author) is interested in exploring the intersection between human rights work and storytelling. She hopes to continue to understand the way people are righting injustice. Her background is in literature and human rights work, and she loves working on pretty much anything narrative-driven and/or cause related. She has traveled to or lived in more than 30 countries on four continents, so stories about travel or communicating cross-culturally get extra points.

SOFÍA AGUILAR (author) is a Chicana writer based in Los Angeles, California. Her work has appeared in the *New Orleans Review*, *Emerge Literary Journal*, and *Melanin Magazine*, among other publications. As an alum of WriteGirl and a first-generation college graduate, Sofía earned a BA from Sarah Lawrence College, where she received the Andrea Klein Willison Prize for Poetry and the Spencer Barnett Memorial Prize for Excellence in Latin American and Latinx Studies. Additionally, she was the Sandra Cisneros Fellow at Under the Volcano in 2022.

STORY HEMI-MOREHOUSE (author and illustrator) is a Māori writer and illustrator for children's media. Often, the focus of her work has been to revitalize and celebrate her Polynesian culture, as well as to create meaningful work that Indigenous children can see themselves in.

SYDNEE MONDAY (author) is a sentimental former child, eldest daughter, and children's book editor. She received a degree in media, journalism, and film from Howard University. Her writing has appeared in places like National Public Radio and *Washington City Paper*.

TATYANA WHITE-JENKINS (author) is a writer, poet, and storyteller from Gloucester, Virginia. Growing up, she was fascinated with the written word and how it provided an avenue for honest storytelling. She later moved to the DC area to turn her passion into a career in communications, using writing and other media platforms to tell the captivating stories of others. After discovering her love for poetry and personal essays, Tatyana is finally ready to tell her own. You can follow her journey on Instagram @tatyanawrites or at tatyanawhitejenkins.com.

ABOUT ROOM TO READ

Room to Read is proud and honored to share the inspiring stories of girls who have defied the odds to create positive change for themselves and their communities. The stories we have contributed to this book—of Dewmini, Sapana, Trang, and Yashika—feature participants in our Girls' Education Program. This program promotes gender equality by keeping girls successfully engaged in school and helping them develop the life skills they need to gain agency over their own lives. We know that with a quality education and mentorship, girls can grow into fulfilled women, reaching heights they never thought possible. Frequently, our Girls' Education Program graduates become pillars of their communities—from educators and health care professionals to business owners and policy makers.

In addition to advancing gender equality, Room to Read promotes literacy in communities experiencing deep educational and economic inequities. We work with educators to support literacy instruction by providing training and instructional materials; partnering with schools to establish and manage children's libraries; and creating, publishing, and distributing children's books in local languages. You can find examples of these books at www.literacycloud.org.

Since our inception in 2000, Room to Read has benefited millions of children in more than 20 countries, including Bangladesh, Cambodia, Grenada, Honduras, India, Indonesia, Italy, Jordan, Laos, Myanmar, Nepal, Pakistan, Philippines, Rwanda, South Africa, Sri Lanka, Tanzania, Uganda, United States, Vietnam, and Zambia. Learn more at www.roomtoread.org.

Room to Read®

ILLUSTRATORS

Eighty-two extraordinary women and nonbinary artists who come from all over the world created the portraits of the trailblazing Rebel figures in this book.

AMY PHELPS, USA, 75, 89
Amy is a children's illustrator based in Portland, Oregon. When they're not making fun, colorful art, they love to get cozy with a good story and a cup of tea.

ANGELA ACEVEDO PEREZ, PERU, 29
Angela is a graduate of arts and business graphic design. She currently works as an illustrator, developing numerous projects for brands that require pieces full of emotion, innovation, and creativity. Through art, she has been able to find her passion, leaving her essence in each work. She has recently designed illustrations for brands such as Juguete Pendiente, Rebel Girls, and Editorial Planeta.

ANGELA HIRE, MEXICO, 85
Angela is a Mexican illustrator who likes to express the love she has for Mexican culture, women, and biodiversity in all her illustrations, leaning on digital and mixed media.

ANNA DIXON, USA, 121, 193
Anna Dixon is a fresh face in illustration who uses her work as a way of connecting people. She's a die-hard Swiftie, a dog lover, and she drives a demin-blue Volkswagon Bug.

ANNALISA VENTURA, ITALY, 45
Annalisa is an illustrator and graphic designer based in Milan. Her works explore the dimension of colors in soft brushstrokes, details, and romantic plays of light that reflect her personality.

AVANI DWIVEDI, INDIA, 167, 169
Avani is an illustrator from Mumbai, India. Through her colorful and whimsical illustrations, she aims to uncover narratives regarding the complex and diverse heritage of India which are yet to be discovered in children's literature.

BANDANA TULACHAN, NEPAL, 177
Bandana is an illustrator and designer from Kathmandu, Nepal. She illustrates and writes children's books and comics and works on illustration, print and publishing projects. Her debut picture book as an author, *Sanu and the Big Storm*, was published by Fineprint Books in 2015. Bandana enjoys traveling, sewing, and scribbling in her journal.

BETSY FALCO, UNITED KINGDOM, 19
Betsy (they/she) is a queer artist working in the east of England. She is a self-taught digital illustrator with a love for mythology/folklore, fantasy, and cowboys. Her artistic strengths are character design and concept illustration with a retro fantasy twist.

CAMELIA PHAM, VIETNAM, 25, 123
Camelia is known for using the human body to tell stories with bold outlines in strong colors, geometry, and kaleidoscopic textures.

CATHY HOGAN, IRELAND, 33
Cathy is an illustrator and designer based in Cork, Ireland. She has illustrated for numerous brands and national campaigns. She enjoys capturing the vibrancy and personality of people in her work.

DANIELLE ELYSSE MANN, USA, 17
Danielle has created cover art, illustrations for children's books, and character designs for a children's clothing line, among other design work. She supports representation for the historically marginalized, especially women of color, and explores this as a narrative in her art practice.

DOMINIQUE RAMSEY, USA, 191
Dominique is an award-winning illustrator who loves drawing whimsical things. She has worked for Pinterest, Snapchat, Penguin Random House, Netflix, and more.

EMMA ACOSTA, USA, 23
Emma is a young illustrator with a passion for all things creative. She spends her time conversing with her pet rocks and pine cones, none of which seem to have an interest in contributing to any conversation.

EVELYN KANDIN GELER, ARGENTINA, 111
Evelyn is a graphic designer and feminist illustrator. She has worked with different brands, NGOs, and entities in relation to women's and human rights and media representation.

GABY VERDOOREN, USA, 131, 187
Gaby is an illustrator who lends herself largely to the nostalgia of her childhood and the strong mystique of the natural world. Her work draws from autumnal color palettes, vintage fantasy aesthetics, and the occult.

GRACE LANKSBURY, UNITED KINGDOM, 163
Grace is a freelance illustrator based in South East London. Working digitally, she creates illustrations that often center around a narrative, whether it's in the form of a book or even just a single illustration. She enjoys playing with color and tone, and her work is characteristically bold and atmospheric.

HAFSA SALOOJEE, CANADA, 129
Hafsa is 16 years old. She lives in Ottawa with her two cats. Her interests include K-Pop and her new mechanical pencil.

ISIP XIN, USA, 95
Isip is an editorial illustrator from the United States. Her work uses bold colors and high energy to tell stories, often featuring beauty, fantasy, and femininity.

IZZY EVANS, UNITED KINGDOM, 49
Izzy is an illustrator and sometimes author of children's books and comics. Their trademark style is known for its diverse characters and atmospheric colors.

JAMIE GREEN, USA, 109
Jamie is a maker and freelance book illustrator living in Greenville (funny, right?), South Carolina. Her goal is to both intrigue and educate, while combining nature and whimsy and creating a space for curiosity (as well as a bit of magic). She is intrigued by themes of human connection, travel, history, and movement.

JANICE CHANG, USA, 27, 113
Janice is a Los Angeles-born and raised illustrator based in Brooklyn, New York. Much of her work takes on an honest representation of the sometimes humorous and bendy limbs of her characters as a way to engage in conversations around social and interpersonal issues.

JENIN MOHAMMED, USA, 69
Jenin is an author and illustrator from Orlando, Florida. She entered the world of children's literature when she won the first SCBWI Summer Spectacular portfolio showcase.

JIALEI SUN, CHINA, 173, 189
Jialei is an illustrator and children's product developer. After completing her MFA in illustration practice from Maryland Institute College of Art, she is now working on creating colorful, characterful, and humorous illustrations that can tell a story.

JIAQI WANG, USA, 47
Jiaqi is a Chinese-born, Los Angeles-based illustrator and animator. She loves using strong lines with equal weight, surrounding flat colors, giving equal priority to every element in a drawing, sometimes using perspective, quirky characters, and moving images to add more to the narrative.

JIAWEN CHEN, CHINA, 21, 93
Jiawen is a freelance illustrator currently based in Guangzhou, China. She prefers to compose her creations with abstract ideas.

JOANNE DERTILI, GREECE, 65
Joanne was born in Greece but has lived in the United Kingdom since 2011. She has worked extensively in animation and also does storyboarding, concept art, 3D painting, and print design.

JULIETTE TOMA, USA, 91
Juliette is an illustrator living in Los Angeles. She's inspired by vintage fashion, old cookbooks, kitsch knickknacks, and strong women.

JUNETIEN, VIETNAM, 101, 201
JuneTien graduated from Kingston University London in 2018 with an MA in visual communication. Since then, she started working as an illustrator and an art educator.

KAMO FRANK, SOUTH AFRICA, 59
Kamo's work exudes visual storytelling of women's excellence with illustrations packed with personality, nostalgia, and vibrancy.

KATHERINE AHMED, USA, 55
Katherine was born and raised in New York. She earned a BA in history and illustration at the New School. In 2021, she was awarded the We Need Diverse Books Illustration Mentorship. She lives in New Jersey with her husband and two daughters.

KELSEE THOMAS, USA, 53
Kelsee is a freelance illustrator working in Los Angeles and originally from Dayton, Ohio. She spends her time listening to too much music, binging Netflix nightly, and trying to finish the books she keeps buying for her ever-growing library.

KIRAN JOAN, USA, 51

Kiran is a Baltimore-based illustrator whose work is characterized by textures and contrasting fluid lines. Her magical worlds are influenced by the mix of cultures she grew up in: Oman, India, and the United States. She has worked with a variety of clients like the *New York Times*, *Politico*, *Huffington Post*, NBC News, and more.

KITT THOMAS, USA, 125

Kitt (Katelan) is a first generation Saint Lucian American author and illustrator whose mission is to celebrate Black culture and encourage diversity in art. They have worked with companies such as Netflix, Hasbro, and Cartoon Network.

LAURA PROIETTI, ITALY, 73

Laura is a children's illustrator, who has done work for a number of publishing houses, Italian and foreign. She has also published various books. Her greatest passion is drawing, accompanied by a love for cats, flowers, and mushrooms.

LU ANDRADE, ECUADOR, 79

Lu is an illustrator from the mountains of Quito. A feminist and a cat lover, she has worked with different clients around the world.

LUCY NIGHTINGALE, AUSTRALIA, 37

Lucy is an Australian high school student who loves to create digital art, particularly portraits. She also enjoys playing hockey, violin and playing with her dog.

LYNNE HARDY, USA, 83

Lynne is a Diné artist from Arizona. She creates modern, illustrated depictions of her Native American culture for all to enjoy and runs an online business named Ajoobaasani. When she is not designing or drawing, she is spending time with her family.

MAEDEH MOSAVERZADEH, IRAN, 159

Maedeh is an Iranian visual artist and illustrator. She currently lives in Calgary, Alberta, and enjoys drawing nature, people, and animals.

MAJU BENGEL, BRAZIL, 105

Maju is a Brazilian illustrator and designer who has worked with a variety of brands and publishers from Brazil and other countries.

MALIHA ABIDI, UNITED KINGDOM, 153

Maliha Abidi is an artist, author, and activist. She has written and illustrated three books—all focused on women's rights, BIPOC stories, and immigrant stories.

MARELLA MOON ALBANESE, USA, 141

Born in Western New York, Marella is currently working out of Brooklyn. She earned her BFA in illustration at the Fashion Institute of Technology. Her inspirations are drawn from the subcultures that arose around reggae, soul, punk, and androgyny, as well as the art of the '50s and '60s.

MARU SALEM-VARGAS, PHILIPPINES, 63

Maru is a children's book illustrator from the Philippines. She loves to share the beauty of the world through her creations.

MELISA FERNÁNDEZ NITSCHE, ARGENTINA, 181

Melisa is an illustrator, graphic designer, and creative artist born and raised in Buenos Aires, Argentina. She currently works freelance accompanied by her cat and a delicious coffee. Her work has been featured in advertisements, children's games, and digital media. Melisa is interested in stories that convey tenderness, sensitivity, and imagination.

MIA SAINE, USA, 39

Mia is a nonbinary Black illustrator and designer from Memphis, Tennessee. They enjoy normalizing and amplifying the empowerment and happiness of minorities and their experiences.

MIA JOELY TUÑÓN, USA, 35

Mia is a 16-year-old high school student from Miami, Florida, who mainly enjoys oil painting and creating digital illustrations with lots of detail and color. As she continues to grow and explore her techniques, Mia would eventually like to display her work in her own art gallery.

MICHELE MILLER, USA, 135

Michele is a 22-year-old, up-and-coming digital illustrator and animator. She is known for her semi-realistic girly pop art style and trying to include diversity in her art and animations.

MONET ALYSSA, USA, 103

Monet Alyssa is a freelance illustrator based in Buffalo, New York. Her work combines digital and traditional media to create psychedelic and colorful motifs that adorn her figures.

NAKI NARH, UNITED KINGDOM, 185, 203

Naki is an artist of Ghanaian descent from two homes: Accra and London. Her work currently plays with explosions of colour and patterns as distinctive features that mark a rapidly evolving signature style. These ideas are expressed through the media of ink and acrylic on paper, digital painting, and canvas.

NATALIA AGATTE, BRAZIL, 67
Natalia is a Brazilian illustrator who loves working with colors, textures, and light to portray diversity in womanhood, with a little bit of fashion. For the past seven years, she's been living in Brooklyn, New York, where she works as a freelance illustrator.

NATALIA CARDONA PUERTA, USA, 205
Natalia Cardona is an award-winning illustrator and designer based in Portland, Oregon. Originally from Colombia, Natalia spent her childhood surrounded by lush forests, mighty mountains, and roaring rivers. Nowadays, Natalia spends her time at her cozy studio creating everything from children's books, large scale art installations, products, and more.

NOA DENMON, USA, 99, 151
Noa is an award-winning illustrator who loves to uplift and depict the stories of the underrepresented and hopes to create work that displays humanity in all its differences.

OLIVIA WALLER, UNITED KINGDOM, 31, 97
Olivia is a Brighton-based freelance illustrator and printmaker, represented by Folio Illustration Agency. She combines elements of collage, drawing, and printmaking within her work to depict scenes of striking characters and celebrations of women.

PAU ZAMRO, MEXICO, 77
Pau is an illustrator from Mexico. Her work is inspired by nature, fantasy, and fashion.

PAULA ZORITE, SPAIN, 43, 161
Paula has worked as an illustrator for many companies and publishers all around the world, such as Capstone, Hinkler, and Pearson. She specializes in digital art and character design.

PHOEBE FALCONER, UNITED KINGDOM, 139
Phoebe Falconer is 15 years old and discovered her passion for art at a very young age. This illustration is her first art commission, and she hopes to go on to do many more!

RACHEL ELEANOR, USA, 107
Rachel has made illustrations for numerous brands, packaging projects, picture books, magazines, stationery, and murals.

RAE CRAWFORD, USA, 71, 81
Rae is an illustrator and designer based in New York City with her partner. She is the creator of the webcomic *I'm Broken, Send Help* and is currently working on her first picture book. Find her on Instagram and Twitter @imbrokencomics.

RAFAELA RIJO-NÚÑEZ, GERMANY, 197, 209
Rafaela is an illustrator who expresses emotions through her images and stories.

REN CAPACIO, PHILIPPINES, 211
Ren is a public health undergraduate with a passion for sharing their love and knowledge for science, wellness, and health through illustration.

ROCIO CAPUTO, ARGENTINA, 117, 127
Rocío is passionate about telling stories through her illustrations and creating deep visual narratives with bright colors and unique textures.

RONIQUE ELLIS, JAMAICA, 137
Ronique is a Jamaican illustrator currently based in New York City. She grew up drawing, reading, and exploring the countryside in a small town.

SARAH MAXWELL, UNITED KINGDOM, 41
Sarah is an American comic artist and illustrator based in London. Her work ranges from fashion illustration to animated GIFs and comics. She loves pastels, flowers, and delicate things.

SANNA LEGAN, USA, 183
Sanna is an activist and artist, with her practice focused around women's rights, discussing issues such as eating disorders, abortion rights, cosmetic surgery, menstruation rights, and other injustices. She has collaborated with the National Women's Health Network, EMILY's List, and Dressember, and is currently the creative director of AmplifyHerNYC, as well as a sex education artist for Planned Parenthood.

SARA CANSINO, MEXICO, 149
Sara is an illustrator who studied marketing and communications and is based in Mexico. She has illustrated for Flamantes libro de Artistas, Revista Cultural, and Epektasi.

SELAH POTMA, USA, 115
Selah has been drawing since she could hold a pencil. She enjoys reading fantasy books and graphic novels, watching TV, frogs, and memes.

SHIANE SALABIE, USA, 61
Shiane is a Jamaican-born illustrator who enjoys telling stories through her art and using bold colors.

SIBEL BALAC, GERMANY, 179
Sibel is a freelance illustrator based in Stuttgart, Germany. Characteristics of her work are a playful style, bold lines, and trendy colors. She loves to focus on different shapes and proportions, especially with her characters. Her illustrations are used for various fields such as editorial, advertising, and animation.

SOFIA CAVALLARI, ITALY, 199
Sofia is an illustrator from Italy, who studied illustration in Rome and in London. Her passions include literature, music, nature, and anything that sparks imagination and creativity. She works as a freelancer and is now publishing her thesis.

SOL COTTI, ARGENTINA, 57

Sol is an award-winning illustrator based in Buenos Aires who likes to tell visual and fresh stories inspired by gender, women, and diversity, using a bold and loose style. Her work has been published in world-renowned publications such as the *New York Times*, *New Yorker*, and *Time* magazine, and for clients like Adidas, Airbnb, and the United Nations. The Guggenheim Museum and Louvre Museum have each featured her work in their promotions.

STORY HEMI-MOREHOUSE, NEW ZEALAND, 195

Story is a Māori writer and illustrator for children's media. Often, the focus of her work has been to revitalize and celebrate her Polynesian culture, as well as to create meaningful work that Indigenous children can see themselves in.

TAINA LAYLA CUNION, USA, 133, 175

Taina is an Afro-Puerto Rican freelance Illustrator from Baltimore, Maryland, illustrating children's books, making comics, and drawing doodles.

TAMIKI, PERU, 165

Tamiki is a Peruvian-Nikkei illustrator and anime lover. She has participated in several art contests, art exhibitions, and cultural projects. She considers that her artwork has the power of generating positive changes and motivating people through the messages of all the characters, themes, and stories being an inspiration and leaving a mark in those who observe it.

TASNEEM AMIRUDDIN, INDIA, 207, 213

Tasneem is a multi-disciplinary illustrator who's inspired by gorgeous pink sunsets, mischievous children, dark nights and bright stars, magic, and other such whimsies. She has illustrated children's picture books and young adult titles for various publishers globally.

TAYLOR MCMANUS, USA, 87

Taylor is an illustrator and educator currently based in northern Virginia. Her work is inspired by photography, fashion, music, film, and pop culture.

TONI D. CHAMBERS, USA, 143

Toni is an illustrator and graphic novelist from New Haven, Connecticut.

TYLER MISHÁ BARNETT, USA, 215

Tyler is a Los Angeles-based illustrator and designer. Her creative mantra is "design with empathy." She specializes in creating vibrant artwork filled with texture and color.

VIVIENNE SHAO, UNITED KINGDOM, 155

Vivienne is a London-based illustrator. She graduated with a masters in illustration and visual media from London College of Communication in 2021.

WEITONG MAI, UNITED KINGDOM, 157

Weitong provides illustrations for both editorial and commercial uses. Her clients include DK Books, Kiehl's, National Trust, Apple, and Moleskine.

YEGANEH YAGHOOBNEZHAD, IRAN, 119

Yeganeh became an illustrator because she has loved drawing since her childhood. Her works stem from ordinary moments, emotions, details, movement, and her life itself.

YIYI CHEN, CHINA, 145

Yiyi is an illustrator who was born in China and studied art at Savannah College of Art and Design in Savannah, Georgia. She is inspired by the interesting shapes and colors of the houses in Savannah.

ZAHRA SOLTANIAN, IRAN, 171

Zahra is a freelancer and she's ranked first in several children's illustration and drawing festivals in Iran.

ZUZA KAMIŃSKA, POLAND, 147

Zuzanna is a Polish illustrator living in Berlin. Her art often includes striking characters and celebrations of women.

REBEL GiRLS App ®

LISTEN TO MORE EMPOWERING STORIES ON THE REBEL GIRLS APP

Download the app to listen to beloved Rebel Girls stories, as well as brand-new tales of extraordinary women. Filled with the adventures and accomplishments of women from around the world and throughout history, the Rebel Girls app is designed to entertain, inspire, and build confidence in listeners everywhere.

PLUS, FIND QR CODES THROUGHOUT THIS BOOK THAT UNLOCK UNFORGETTABLE AUDIO STORIES!

MORE FROM REBEL GIRLS

Let the stories of more real-life women entertain and inspire you. Each volume in the Good Night Stories series includes 100 tales of extraordinary women.

Check out these mini books too! Each one contains 25 tales of talented women, along with quizzes and engaging activities.

Dig deeper into the lives of these five real-life heroines
with the Rebel Girls chapter book series.

Learn the exciting business
of Madam C.J. Walker, the
hair care industry pioneer
and first female self-made
millionaire in the US.

Uncover the groundbreaking
inventions of Ada Lovelace,
one of the world's first
computer programmers.

Explore the thrilling
adventures of Junko Tabei,
the first female climber to
summit Mount Everest.

Follow the awe-inspiring
career of Alicia Alonso,
a world-renowned prima
ballerina from Cuba.

Discover the inspiring story
of Dr. Wangari Maathai,
the Nobel Peace Prize–winning
environmental activist
from Kenya.

The quirky questions in these books
help curious readers explore their
personalities, forecast their futures, and
find common ground with extraordinary
women who've come before them.

ABOUT REBEL GIRLS

REBEL GIRLS is a global, multi-platform empowerment brand dedicated to helping raise the most inspired and confident generation of girls through content, experiences, products, and community. Originating from an international best-selling children's book, Rebel Girls amplifies stories of real-life women throughout history, geography, and field of excellence. With a growing community of nearly 20 million self-identified Rebel Girls spanning more than 100 countries, the brand engages with Generation Alpha through its book series, award-winning podcast, events, and merchandise. With the 2021 launch of the Rebel Girls app, the company has created a flagship destination for girls to explore a wondrous world filled with inspiring true stories of extraordinary women.

Join the Rebel Girls' community:
Facebook: facebook.com/rebelgirls
Instagram: @rebelgirls
Twitter: @rebelgirlsbook
Web: rebelgirls.com
App: rebelgirls.com/app

If you liked this book, please take a moment to review it wherever you prefer!